Stranger in the Pew

Stranger in the Pew

KENNETH WRAY CONNERS

Judson Press, Valley Forge

STRANGER IN THE PEW

For
CHRISTINE
who practices while others preach

Contents

Introduction

A special value of *Stranger in the Pew* is the authentic experience out of which the author writes. Kenneth Conners has participated in, suffered with, and lived through the events described so graphically in this book. For many years he himself stood in the shoes of the friend to whom these letters are addressed. He knows well the foibles and follies of congregations and individual Christians, and he writes sympathetically of the drastic need for changes in the church. His book issues a most effective invitation to those church members who have been in the church's membership but not of its mission to make the journey Mr. Conners himself has made—from passenger to member of the crew.

As important as the credential of firsthand personal experience is the fact that Mr. Conners writes from the perspective of a church "pillar." He writes from the inside of the institutional church as one who wants to conserve whatever is of value in its heritage while at the same time letting its hope take wing. He is a member of the "establishment" church creatively and courageously working to enable it to respond to the needs and imperatives of the modern era. Both conservative and liberal churchmen will identify with Mr. Conners' concern to honor both change and continuity in the work of the church and his clear affirmation that servanthood, not success, is the criterion of the church's fidelity to its gospel. Most appealing is his compassion for people who are so upset by the inevitable changes that they have a difficult time coping with them.

Mr. Conners has a hard time coping with change himself. Anyone deeply rooted in the Christian community does, if he lives by memory as well as hope. Mr. Conners couldn't have written this book ten, or even five, years ago. His own thinking has changed significantly over those years. In my opinion, a great many church members across the country will have to undergo a similar change of mind if the church is to be both relevant and faithful in the years ahead. This book is an excellent guide for the "church pillar" who is willing to undergo the changes of insight and commitment required for effective Christian living in the modern day.

The church is struggling for integrity of identity and vocation in a revolution which it can neither control nor predict. We don't know what the church will look like fifty years from now. Although it is interesting to speculate on such matters, Mr. Conners' book does something more immediately useful. He gives practical suggestions as to how faith may be deepened and sharpened today for witness in the tomorrows. How does one begin to read the Bible with insight? How does one start and develop a small study or mission group? How does one "make" a retreat? How does an "establishment" congregation struggle to find a new style of work and worship appropriate to its changing urban environment? These and similar questions are given wise attention out of Mr. Conners' rich personal experience.

It has been my privilege to be one of the pastors of the congregation in which Mr. Conners has served as Lay Leader in recent years. Whatever is at present healthy, creative, and strong about this congregation bears the mark of his contribution. Ever seeking to reconcile those alienated by change, while taking part in the alienating changes himself, Ken Conners has been friend and counselor to pastors and parishioners alike, helping to make friends of many a stranger in the pew.

ROBERT RAINES

January, 1970

"Sure It's Your Life . . . But Is It?"

Dear Wayne:

You really shook me up last evening. It's not that your words filled me with surprise or suddenly gave me a new insight into your state of mind! During our many years of friendship I have sensed from your frequent negative comments and your apparent resignation to a grim sort of fatalism that life for you was something more to be endured than enjoyed.

What most disturbed me, I suppose, was hearing you so flatly voice your futility. I felt as though I were a physician attending a desperately ill patient, endeavoring to provide him with the reassurance to encourage him to continue the struggle for life, only to hear him murmur, with a resignation born of despair, that he honestly doesn't want to live any longer.

If I can recall your words, they went something like this: "Ken, when I hear you talk about leading retreats, going to various churches as a lay preacher, see the gleam in your eyes, and hear the excitement in your voice, I am very happy for you. You certainly will enjoy retirement when that day comes. As for me, I just can't believe there is a God. From everything I observe, based on my education and engineering training, I don't see anything but absurdity in the world we live in and the life we lead." And then, wistfully, you blurted out those heartbreaking words: "It must be wonderful to believe in something!"

11

From a personal point of view, Wayne, your words filled me with sadness because you really possess (if you will forgive the expression!) a God-given potential for creativity and happiness. This, I am convinced, is the fact all of us should recognize about ourselves. One of the purposes of this life is to learn how to free ourselves from the bondage of self, so that we can live for others in the liberating dimension of Christian maturity.

Your words also disturbed me because you are a member of a Christian church, yet an atheist. You are active in your church; yet Christ has never penetrated your life—which is true of thousands of churchgoers. It is an inevitable result of our namby-pamby approach to Christianity. The attitude of church people often is defensive, almost timid, as though Jesus Christ were someone to be apologized for as a starry-eyed dreamer, out of step with today's cynical world. As a result, most ministers make few if any demands upon those seeking admission to their churches. They are so eager to add names to their rolls—to acquire a reputation for having a growing parish—that they welcome the prospective new member on his own terms. Actually it is easier to join a church than almost any other organization. In your own church a new member simply inscribes his name in your membership book. Then, just last week, I heard one of your long-time members exclaim: "Dammit! The young people coming into our church today don't believe in anything. They're heathen! I don't know why they join."

Well, I can tell him why such people join your church and many other churches. It is because in our country today church membership is a superficial sign of being a "Good Guy," a basis for social acceptance. Church membership entitles parents to take their children to receive so-called instruction for about forty-five minutes every Sunday, as if this would immunize little Johnny and Mary against the sins of society and keep them from being contaminated by some of the less savory ethical and moral practices they encounter in the adult world (often in their own homes). Yet we say we don't believe in miracles!

Today more people belong to churches than to country clubs and fraternal organizations, but only for some very shoddy reasons. For one thing, the dues are lower. Where else can you set your own assessment and pay—or not pay—according to a whim? Also, there is no obligation to attend regularly, as there is, for example, for members of the local Rotary Club. There's no obligation to study and grow in understanding, as there is if you join the Masons and move up through their various degrees and orders. Affiliating with a church is akin to getting a visa on a passport; without it, an ambitious individual finds it exceedingly difficult to travel far in political life, in the professions, and often in business. It really is shocking to contemplate how glibly, how irreverently, we identify ourselves as "Christians," and how brashly we appropriate all the status and respectability that the term implies, with little or no concern for the demands that should be met before we so much as dare to apply that appellation to ourselves.

In an even larger sense, Wayne, your words last night really shook me up because they typify our ethos today. Wherever we look, we see mass cynicism, a feeling that life is meaningless, a disillusionment with former values and standards, yet an unwillingness to adopt meaningful new values. We see frustration-driven people having recourse to excessive use of alcohol. We see millions of people lured by mass media vainly seeking a satisfying life through all sorts of bogus passports to an exotic tomorrow: charm courses, glamour cosmetics, conspicuous spending, the winning ticket at the race track. We recognize much extramarital experimentation in both suburbs and slums, either because life is so secure that it becomes dull, or so grim that it has no "kicks." We find others indulging in psychedelic drugs to effect a dreamlike escape in a search for fulfillment that some consider to be religiously motivated. On a more optimistic note, we've seen idealistic young people going into the Peace Corps in an effort to find meaning in life.

It seems to me that the crux of your situation is really your inability to believe. I don't mean that you obstinately reject God. Essentially, you are a religious person. Inwardly you yearn for something—assurance, hope, ultimate reality—which intellectually you refuse to accept. Quite understandably this colors your entire life. It makes you reluctant to venture, to take risks, to make leaps of faith. In other words, it's not the external world but *you* who have rendered yourself ineffective. You are like a motorist who has lost his way but who refuses to trust road maps, in spite of seeing other drivers with road maps proceeding faithfully along various highways. You have shifted your mental gears into neutral and drifted in whatever direction and at whatever speed external circumstances permit.

Perhaps after you have read my harsh words about church people and the institution itself, you will ask why I have anything to do with the church. Certainly, you might logically infer that I am down on all formal expressions of religion. But I am not. Actually, I love the church. Here and there, amidst all the sloth of ministers and lay people, I can actually discern some wonderful things happening. In a sense, I look upon the church as a father looks upon a son who is capable of great things; that is, with love and affection but also with sorrow and heartache, because in his youthful anxiety for public approbation he has lowered his standards, surrendered many of his ideals, and generally made a fool of himself! And, like an adolescent who wants to make his mark, the church must realize that if it is to transform the world, it first must reform itself and become an instrument of dynamic leadership, without compromise or vacillation. It must attain some decent measure of responsible adulthood, based on self-discipline, selfless dedication, and realistic involvement with the world's people and problems.

Now why, Wayne, am I writing to you rather than sitting down and chatting about our respective philosophies of life? I believe you know the answer. It is because we haven't been able, in the past, to have any meaningful dialogue on this important subject. For instance, I can recall one recent conversation which began to be just a bit fruitful when you suddenly warned: "Now don't give me any of that Jesus stuff!" I think you felt threatened; I felt frustrated.

This is all too common a reaction when two people endeavor to talk about a subject which deeply involves their total being—emotional and intellectual, physical and spiritual, temporal and eternal. How unfortunate it is that we mortals are able to discuss the trivial, the inconsequential, the commonplace without diffidence or embarrassment, but we find ourselves reluctant to exchange ideas on the really vital concerns which are of life-and-death importance! And yet I sense a hunger among people to come to grips with questions concerning the true meaning of life. How ironic it is that the very people who are most starved for spiritual sustenance and are intellectually the best equipped to explore creatively the deep dimensions of existence are the ones most likely to shun contact with the organized church! To them, church people too often seem starry-eyed and sentimental, shallow and superficial, smug and self-righteous, intellectually stuffy and sterile, self-centered and self-indulgent, or sectarian and straitlaced. Let's face it, Wayne: too often they are right. These sensitive persons who never attend public worship constitute what the late Paul Tillich called the "latent church." They need the church, and the church needs them. But only an earnest congregation of creative, committed Christians can attract them.

The other obstacle to meaningful dialogue between us has been the sort of barrier Reuel Howe has so well delineated in his book *The Miracle of Dialogue.** One of these barriers is language itself. You are

*Footnote information is found on pages 127-128.

an engineer, and you speak of logarithms, sine waves, cross-modulation, sinusoidal forces, hysteresis, and other terms which convey real meaning only to other engineers. In much the same way, theologians too often lose the common touch by talking about such ideas as the incarnation, hermeneutics, transcendence, eschatology, and other matters which seem remote from our daily lives. Thus language, which is supposed to be a vehicle for communication, actually inhibits the interchange of ideas.

Images are another barrier to dialogue. Whenever the subject of religion arises, I suspect you have a childhood image of some old-time evangelist pointing a finger at you and demanding to know, in a voice quavering with emotion, whether you are "saved." Therefore, before any words even are uttered, you feel that you can discern the direction which the dialogue is about to take. Accordingly, you either cut off the conversation or erect an emotional barrier which prevents you from hearing the words.

Again, a feeling of anxiety may arise because you fear that the misconceptions and prejudices which, through the years, have shielded your point of view from the onslaught of new and threatening ideas are about to be stripped away. This leads inevitably to defensiveness. None of us likes to have a comfortable mind-set placed in jeopardy. That is the reason we have never made any real progress in exploring together the meaning of life.

Now, in writing to you, Wayne (I hope you are still reading!), I don't intend to preach. I do want to respect your personal integrity. I want to acknowledge that you have a right to believe that there is no meaning to life, just as I have a right to believe that there is. But I want to share with you a few of the things I have discovered during the past nine years because of the great change that an awakened faith in God has made in my life.

I, too, used to be dominated by a negative point of view. My personal effectiveness was woefully diminished by a feeling of inadequacy. I was functioning on perhaps 10 percent of the potential that God had given me. But I found that in man's search to know both himself and God (as Bultmann pointed out, it is impossible to know one without knowing the other!) the key to the mystery is Jesus Christ. The more one learns of Christ, his life, and his teachings, the more spiritually sensitive one becomes. As daily events occur, alternative avenues of action begin to appear, avenues which were veiled before but now loom before us with challenging clarity. The idea of obedience takes possession of our thinking. Confronted, perhaps for the first time, with the choice of doing what we, selfishly, want to do or what God really expects of us, we feel a new tension, born of the conflict of interests. We find that trying to follow Christ is far from easy. We see what a disturbing threat he becomes to a complacent way of life. It dawns upon us that only through losing our life—our old ego-centered existence—can we be freed to live creatively and find the true life that God wants for each of us.

All of this doesn't sound like a prescription for "peace of mind," does it? Or a panacea for escape from reality? On the contrary, it offers, in exchange for the cheap and often tawdry pleasures of our rat-race mode of life, something infinitely richer and more satisfying—the joy which comes of living responsibly for others.

But how do we do this? How do we find God's will? How do we learn to recognize the imperatives which Christ has put before us? And how do these things relate to the conventional church with all its obvious faults and weaknesses?

I see by the clock that it's growing late, and I fear I may already have presumed on your good nature in this letter. Indeed, you may be scowling right now and grumbling to yourself: "It's *my* life. It's *my* business how I live it. By what right does *he* butt into my affairs?"

Sure, it's your life . . . but is it?

You didn't create it. You didn't ask to be born. You came into a world which already existed—a natural world of amazing scope and complexity, which functions in an orderly way according to timeless laws and in response to an amazing cosmic intelligence. So why are you here? What is the purpose of your life? Where and how can you find meaning and continuity and fulfillment?

I happen to believe that your life is *not* your own, nor does my life belong to me. If you are willing to respond to this letter and continue our "dialogue" on paper, I can share with you some of the practices and techniques which, for me at least, have opened doors to a new life that is more vibrant than any I knew before.

Faithfully,

Ken

"What Have You Done for Me Recently?"

Dear Wayne:

How pleased I was to receive your letter! Of course you are uneasy when you are confronted with ideas which are alien to your thinking! But let's push ahead. At least I have stimulated some sharp questions from you—about the clergy, about churches, about the hypocrisy of so many who pose as being religious.

Before we exchange ideas on any of these, accept my sincere thanks for opening yourself to me and being willing to put up with my rambling thoughts. Where we ultimately will arrive, I don't know. But need we care? In your engineering experiments, I'm sure you frequently embark on programs with only a vague notion of your destination. But you proceed "in faith," and the outcome, no doubt, often amazes you. In fact, faith is an essential and *priceless* ingredient of *all* life. Without it, we just couldn't launch forth on any venture.

You raise a pertinent question when you ask: "How did the church in America get so deeply into trouble? In my church, we have more dissension than I can ever remember. People are touchy, prone to jump to false conclusions, and easily irritated! Why, we even have teams of lay people traveling from house to house to meet with groups of our members to try to heal wounds."

I suspect that to understand the situation confronting the church today we must turn back the pages of history a few generations and observe the beginning of a sad phenomenon. We are witnesses of the spectacle of an institution whose avowed mission it is to transform society but which now permits that society, instead, to mold the church into conformity with *its* standards.

Long before the urban population explosion, the church in rural areas, towns, and smaller cities had its roots in the local parish. Here lived a cross section of white, Anglo-Saxon America. Congregations were drawn from a broad spectrum: farmers, laboring people, clerks, a large number of white-collar business and professional people, and a few people of wealth. Non-whites generally had their own churches. Non-Anglo-Saxons felt at home in the Roman Catholic church.

The Protestant church of this period was inherently stable. People seldom moved away. It was not unusual for a church member to be baptized, bound in holy matrimony, and buried, all by the ministry of the same church. Thus the parish became the hub of social life for the worshiping community—a place where rich and poor could rub shoulders and come to know one another.

The level of education of the church membership was rather modest. As a result, the minister usually was looked up to as one of the more highly trained men in the community, on a par with the physician, the lawyer, and the school teacher. Since most colleges were church-founded and church-supported, the minister enjoyed a prestige which enhanced his role of leadership in the community.

All this related the church, in a somewhat subtle way, to the great American dream that a Horatio Alger "rags to riches" career could be within the grasp of any ambitious, diligent young man. Individual initiative was stressed, with stern admonitions regarding personal morality. Social issues, such as child labor, women's suffrage, and the rise of labor unions, were of less concern than the personal evangelization of those who had not accepted Christ. Church people thought of mission only as "taking the gospel to the heathen." In fact, the news that a young person had chosen to give his life to Christ by studying for the ministry, or by enrolling for missionary training, was cause for rejoicing. For how else could one really serve him?

As the years passed, the industrial revolution and the growth of scientific technology created hundreds of thousands of new jobs. Like a magnet, America's northern cities drew their workers from small towns and rural areas, including the vanguard of what was to become a great flow of Negroes from the South. As the nation's agricultural, industrial, and commercial life became more complex, advanced education no longer was a luxury for the privileged, but a necessity for all who aspired to worthwhile careers. Now the average minister saw his parishioners catching up, and often surpassing him, in academic training. Increasingly he found himself faced with issues of social, economic, and political sophistication which placed him at a disadvantage when trying to help his congregation.

Then came two shattering developments which rudely shook American society, and with it, the church. The first was the depression of the 1930s, which not only punctured the average citizen's complacency, but made it brutally clear that man was not the master of his destiny. Scarcely had the nation begun to recover when there came the second shock—World War II. The cream of our youth went abroad, as their fathers had done a generation earlier, to fight to make the world safe for democracy. As the casualty lists lengthened, people felt their dependence upon God more and more. Church attendance increased as people prayed for an end to the spreading conflict. Few dreamed it would lead to Hiroshima and the unleashing of thermonuclear power.

With the cessation of hostilities, material goods poured from America's factories in record volumes. Home construction spurted, and the exodus to the suburbs began. On the periphery of every urban center, real estate subdivisions sprang up, with street after street of monotonously-similar houses. The uniformity of their price tags acted like a filter, admitting into the area a homogeneous influx of white-collar business and professional people who could meet the mortgage payments. Thus were created thousands of "bedroom ghettoes," inhabited by urbanites who spent their leisure time associating largely with mirror-images of themselves.

Sensing a bonanza, the church joined the gold rush to the suburbs, eager to give its ecclesiastical blessing to this unprecedented prosperity. At this time, my own church considered selling our extensive plant to a Negro congregation and erecting a new building in "Utopia." But, thank God, we elected to stand our ground and seek new ways of serving our urban community

As church memberships expanded and budgets soared, it came to be tacitly understood that all the spiritual work of the parish should be handled by the growing staff of professionals. It was not uncommon to find three, four, or more ordained clergymen serving a prosperous church. Although few probably realized it, the Reformation concept of the priesthood of all believers was being replaced by the concept of the clergyman as father and intermediary with God. Generally, lay participation was limited to such church-supporting duties as ushering, property management, fund-raising, and the staging of social activities for the enjoyment of the members. Little else was asked of lay people as long as they footed the bills!

At this time the church appeared to be at its greatest strength. Articles in popular magazines hailed America's religious vitality. Membership hit new highs and attendance set new records. Financial giving reached impressive totals, although per capita giving was disturbingly low in comparison with expenditures for amusements, alcoholic beverages, and cigarettes.

Nevertheless, like a man who outwardly appears to be in radiant health but inwardly harbors a malignancy, the suburban church was rapidly becoming spiritually flabby. Gone was the dream of a servant-church, expending its life for others. Self-centered suburbanites were paying a servant-pastor to devote *his* life to massaging the spiritual backs of his parishioners every time they felt an ache or pain. Thus grew up the cult of the personality minister. Great emphasis was placed on pulpit urbanity. Sermons were judged to be good if they were entertaining, dealt with personal problems in a soothing way, and steered clear of controversy. Because life in the suburbs was pleasant, albeit monotonous, the minister was to avoid, at all costs, any challenge to the status quo. As all members of the community had the same aspirations, attitudes, and antipathies, the church clearly was not to transform society, but to give its blessing to the cult of conformity. Thus evolved the "church neurotic" worshiping its suburban gods, offering its litanies for peace of mind, and singing its congregational refrain: "What have you done for me recently?"

In the meantime, city churches faced a different situation. As the migration to the suburbs continued, the vacuum left behind was swiftly filled by people pouring in from more congested areas. Almost overnight neighborhoods changed, population density climbed, and pockets of extreme poverty began to appear where there had been affluence. The trek to the suburbs often removed from city congregations the people best able to provide leadership. As a result, church membership declined, budgets were cut back, and the urban ministry declined at the very time, and at the very places, where it was most needed. Moreover, denominational officials often assigned inexperienced, unimaginative clergymen to the churches that were in the gravest trouble and needed the most dedicated, capable men available. In virtually every large city, churches either followed their congregations to the suburbs, merged with other communions, or struggled to serve the remnants of a once-active parish, often through financial subsidies by a city missionary society. Here and there, a church still had sufficient resources to mount a creative program designed to reorient its ministry to the changing needs of the city.

But now all congregations, urban and suburban alike, were exposed to new and divisive tensions. Although the civil rights movement won technical victories in the courts and governmental promises of better housing and increased job opportunities, the black man's frustration grew as overcrowding and unemployment failed to abate. Hostile ethnic groups found close contact dangerously abrasive. The white man's fires of annoyance, apprehension, and anger were fanned by "Black Power," civil disobedience, and violence.

As if clashing views on civil rights were not cause enough for dissension, the conflict in Vietnam continued to escalate, dividing church people into two fluttering flocks—hawks and doves. The nation's youth, caught up in the pressures of a social revolution, condemned their elders for making such a mess of things. Vowing to assert their freedom, they embarked on all sorts of conspicuous behavior, from student demonstrations to love-ins. Little wonder that virtually every church member felt trapped in a social upheaval which his denomination seemed to be either promoting, countenancing, or evading.

Prophetically, in 1961, Gibson Winter had declared: "Where Christianity has become identified with upper-class élites, it has lacked a substantial base in the working population and has been unable to weather social change."*

So now the "church neurotic" is well on his way to becoming the "church psychotic."

And why?

Just think of the schizophrenic attitudes which have long separated certain fundamentalistic sects from their liberal "social gospel" brothers. Until recently such divisiveness seemed confined to the Protestant scene, but now it has become visible also in the Roman Catholic church. And how paranoid those attitudes can become under the stress of radical social change!

Hear the cries, Wayne, from the conservatives: "The church should keep its nose out of public issues." "The church should remain aloof from the National Council of Churches, which consorts with churchmen from godless Russia." "We should not get entangled with Catholics or Jews." "We should concentrate on the individual and his salvation." "We must get back to the Bible." "Save a man's soul, and he'll exert a Christian influence through his business, political, and social contacts."

21

"But how can a solitary layman exert sufficient influence in this complex age?" retorts the liberal churchman. "The church must take a stand on public issues, using its resources to sway public opinion through education or, if necessary, through militant action. Only in this way can we restore human dignity to our underprivileged brothers, the very ones whom Christ sought to serve. We've been so concerned about individual salvation that we've shut our eyes to injustice and exploitation."

This issue would be easier to deal with if all church people fitted into one or the other of these ideological camps. But they don't. People can't be categorized quite so neatly, especially at a time when society is undergoing agonizing restructuring. Actually, many of us are liberal with regard to some issues and conservative in our reaction to others. This brings us face to face with a basic question, namely: Is it possible to change society without initially or concurrently changing the individual's personal viewpoint? Unless the hearts of people undergo change, external changes superimposed on our society will provoke resistance, bitterness, frustration, and even violence. This is where the liberal brother stubs his psychological toe. But a change of heart requires time, patience, and forbearance. I believe you've felt this, Wayne, when you've said of some churchmen who have displayed intolerance for the opposition: "Why, they're orthodox liberals!"

Isn't it the church's dual job, then, to sensitize its members to the spiritual values inherent in *all* of life, and at the same time, to make them aware of their responsible stake in collective social action? In manifesting its concern for the individual the church should never permit the prejudices and self-interest of individual members to interfere with its prophetic ministry to the victims of injustice and discrimination. Putting it another way, we must never let *our* concern for the *individual* churchman get in the way of *Christ's* concern for *all* human beings.

But if the church thinks it has weathered this social crisis and can now relax and await a return to "normalcy," let it arouse itself to yet another challenge!

For several years, industry has been quitting urban centers for outlying locations which offer adequate parking and freedom from congestion. As our cities are becoming centers for light manufacturing and for commercial, professional, recreational, and cultural activities, the conventional flow of white-collar commuters from suburbs to city is being countered by a reverse flow of blue-collar factory workers. As industry flees the cities, industrial workers, too, are beginning to follow their work to the outlying areas. Already certain labor leaders (perhaps more alert to the demographic trends than some church officials) show concern about this new migration, principally because industrial workers, who normally vote Democratic, may be converted to Republicanism by the more conservative atmosphere of the suburbs, and thus lose their ardor for unionism.

Now what does this growing migration of industrial workers mean to the church? Simply this: The pressure on the suburbs to open their white, Anglo-Saxon ghettoes to working people of various races, colors, and nationalities will increase relentlessly. Ironically, the city church which once fled to the suburbs may find it has merely postponed its day of confrontation. Then, for a second time it must search its soul and wrestle with one of the basic issues of Christian brotherhood, namely: Is the church to be a place where *all* human beings are welcome and a diversity of backgrounds is permitted to enrich the lives of all who worship together?

But there is another side to the coin. Although this confrontation may be viewed with dismay by some suburban churchgoers, the more creative churchman will see in this an opportunity, a second chance, a reprieve. For now he will have *two* opportunities for Christian witness: First, he may devote some of his time and money to service in the urban community, perhaps through involvement with a church which has remained in the inner city; and second, he may welcome these new neighbors from the city, regardless of their race, and thus help to make of the suburbs a more Christian community.

It may well be that the future of American Protestantism will hinge on how faithfully our suburban clergy and laity meet this new challenge. Can the once-neurotic church, having become a psychotic church, now become transformed into a creative church? Is there, indeed, hope that the institutionalized church may renew itself?

I am convinced that there is. But it depends, perhaps more than we realize, on the sense of direction, urgency, and commitment which the laity has the vision to provide. And when I say "laity," Wayne, *that's us!*

Dr. Robert J. McCracken, minister emeritus of The Riverside Church, tells an amusing story about a dog in a crate on a railway station platform. A waiting passenger, pacing nervously back and forth, noticed the dog and his forlorn demeanor. Turning to a nearby railway attendant, the passenger exclaimed: "My, what an unhappy dog." The attendant agreed, "He *is* unhappy—very unhappy. The poor animal doesn't know where he's come from, or where he's at. And Mister, that's not the worst of it. He's chewed up his destination tag, so he doesn't know where he's bound for, either!"

That, points out Dr. McCracken, is the situation the church finds itself in today.

Wayne, I must end this letter. It's past midnight, and besides, I hear our pet springer spaniel whining and yelping outside, begging to be let in. He sounds apprehensive—almost hysterical—as if he fears we have forgotten him. Someone has said that in the eyes of a dog, man appears to be God. Is there something symbolic in this for us?

Faithfully,

Ken

"You Can't Have Easter Without Good Friday!"

Dear Wayne:

What a catechism of questions you flung at me in your last letter! Apparently my criticism of the typical suburban church and my concern for the desperate situation facing urban congregations led you to believe that the church *per se* is beyond reclaiming, hopelessly out of step with today's needs, and a dying institution. "For," you ask, "how is the layman to find the sort of renewal and new life you speak of? Does he have to go it alone? And if so, how in God's name can he do it? Does he turn to secular humanism? That isn't what you implied in your first letter, when you said you loved the church and had faith in it. I'm confused!"

Wayne, my apologies to you. I realize I have failed to make clear several crucial points. Here they are:

First, renewal of the church is a continuing, never-ending phenomenon. Second, the shape of the "renewed" church gradually emerges from the ashes of the dying church. Third, this shape can be discerned in the response which certain congregations make to Christ's call for a more radical form of servanthood. Fourth, such change requires prophetic leadership on the part of the clergy, and commitment and involvement on the part of the laity. Fifth, renewal comes into being through a covenant type of relationship, wherein a people recaptures the sense of Christian community which characterized the earliest church, accompanied by the power of the Holy Spirit to change lives and alter society.

As we look about us, Wayne, occasionally we can find churches which are beginning to point the way toward a more Christian life. Such churches are seeking to break away from their former preoccupation with self, which I like to call the religious ghetto mentality. Their congregations are realizing that inherently the church of Jesus Christ consists of people and not property; that it exists for service and not status; and that it discovers a new and revitalized life to the extent that it is willing to lose its old life. The structure of the institutional church is thus a means to an end, and not an end in itself. They are discovering that God is to be found not merely in the sanctuary (if, indeed, he is found there at all!) but more often in "the world" at the point of human need: in the kitchen of a slum dwelling, in the ward of a hospital, in a prison cell, in a marriage guidance clinic, and in any place where two or more gather in his name to become agents for healing, helping, and reconciling.

Now there seem to be certain distinguishing marks of the servant church which set it apart from self-serving churches. Let me refer to five of these marks or attributes. But remember, all five may not always be discernible.

First, the servant church opens wide its doors to all, regardless of race, nationality, or economic status. This open-door policy is more than a gesture, or a concession, to minority pressure. Rather it is a recognition that a congregation, if it is to be a genuine fellowship of the concerned, must be nonexclusive and all-inclusive. Only in this way can it broaden its understanding of humanity, deepen its spiritual sensitivity and integrity, and seek to become truly mature in Christ.

Second, such churches have free pulpits where their ministers can preach prophetically, linking Christ's life and teachings with the situations confronting us. With apostolic power, these preachers point to places where the concerned Christian must take a stand, become involved, and help shape a more just, compassionate society. Such preachers inevitably become involved in community affairs, discern the strategies underlying power struggles, and thus combine realism with idealism in appraising the current scene. In their churches there is likely to be experimentation with new forms of worship and liturgies designed to express the great truths of our faith in relevant and significant words, song, and pageantry.

Third, these churches strive to de-emphasize certain superficial aspects of "fellowship" formerly considered important, such as the insipid social groups, club-like organizations, bazaars, and cake sales. Instead, they are fostering a true *koinonia* relationship in which members of the congregation relate to one another on a deeper level, forming a Christian community which in spirit unites people who have diverse backgrounds, ethnic origins, and economic levels, but who have a common love for Christ and a desire to seek God's will for their life together.

Fourth, these churches emphasize study as a prerequisite to an intelligent understanding, not only of our Judeo-Christian heritage, but of the role which a professing Christian must play in society today. Frequently this study starts at the very moment that new people express an interest in exploring membership. They may take part in six or more membership class sessions, with lectures by the ministers, group discussion led by lay people trained in the Christian faith and in group dynamics, and worship together climaxed by the celebration of communion. Or the instruction may be as extensive as at the remarkable Church of the Saviour, in Washington, D.C., where six structured courses are required of every candidate for membership, with present members expected to continue their personal growth by taking such elective courses as Interpretative Speech, Counseling, Christian Classics, History of the Church, Prayer, and Group Dynamics. Elizabeth O'Connor, of the Church of the Saviour, delineates the underlying philosophy which should prevail in training such:

> For the individual student, no creed or theological dogma is memorized, to be glibly recited; rather the student is presented, in present day terminology, the laws of the spirit as taught by Jesus. He is urged to disprove them if he can, but in any case to try them. The point is especially emphasized that, rather than blindly accepting the claim that Jesus is the Son of the Living God or flatly denying it, the student is to try living with Him for six months.*

Central to such a program is, of course, the Bible and related commentaries. Books on theology, philosophy, ethics and interpersonal relations, sociology, and psychology are of great value. Important, too, is exposure to the perceptive insights of contemporary writers of novels, plays, and poetry. Laymen are encouraged to keep abreast of theological trends by reading at least one religious journal like *The Christian Century, Christianity and Crisis, The Commonweal,* or *America.*

Fifth, these churches are realizing that unless the laity is actively engaged in the mission of witnessing and ministering daily to victims of injustice, intolerance, or inhumanity, it simply cannot, in times like these, call itself "Christian." Ministers of such churches look upon their buildings as training centers for equipping laymen for their work in the world. Lay people look upon themselves as a missionary people, called to go out where the waters are deep and the currents often turbulent. Through many personal forms of witness, they put into practice in the laboratory of human relations the principles they learned in classes and seminars.

27

But there is this significant difference: During their preparatory training, they learned intellectually of the Christian faith, but actually they saw only through a glass, darkly. Then, through personal involvement, they began to identify with Christ's compassion, finding themselves face to face with the tremendous reality of God and comprehending at last what it really means to be members of the body of Christ.

Now what is the result of all this? Are these pioneering congregations finding success? Are people flocking to their doors, eager to share in their work? Are they growing in membership, in financial strength? Are their congregations united in dedication to this exciting cause? Are they, in a word, recreating the church of Jesus Christ to the accompaniment of cheers and hosannas?

In the instances I have observed, Wayne, they definitely are not. On the contrary, such churches frequently are in a state of turmoil. Some members become incensed at the temerity of preachers who dare to question the status quo or, even worse, to imply that the church members may share in the common guilt for society's injustices. Many wail that the church has no business sticking its ecclesiastical nose into politics (which, they say, is dirty) or into the problems of the underprivileged (who, they say, are dirty). In resisting change, they stoutly reject Teilhard de Chardin's concept of an evolutionary progression toward ultimate perfection—omega—and instead call to mind Martin Buber's observation that: "In so far as man rests satisfied with the things that he experiences and uses, he lives in the past, and his moment has no present content."*

Caught in the upheaval of our social revolution, conservative members of the typical liberal congregation feel helpless, frustrated, and resentful. To them, the church appears to be a part of a disturbing new power structure. Their resentment and vituperation are likely to be leveled at the minister, the church, or the denominational leaders, who, they feel, don't know what they're talking about.

A schizophrenic phenomenon of this situation is that the very church members who wax most indignant at the use of pressure tactics like picketing, boycotts, and demonstrations by civil rights and other groups now turn to these same tactics to express *their* indignation. As a result, increasing numbers of church members have been registering their dissent by reducing or cutting off their financial support. Others figuratively picket their church by writing angry letters, publishing critical newsletters, and holding meetings to arouse the opposition. Still others petulantly walk out on the church, complaining, "I'll not worship here anymore until this church becomes religious again!"

28

Such actions remind us that the miracle of renewal, rebirth, or resurrection—whether physical or spiritual, personal or corporate—seldom is attained without pain, suffering, and the experience of death. In other words, "We can't have Easter without Good Friday!"

How little these laymen really understand true Christian stewardship! What a distorted concept they have of the nature of the church! How sad it is that they have failed to enter into the sort of *koinonia* relationship in which each member offers and receives understanding, forgiveness, trust, and reconciliation not because he merits it, but because this is the gift of the Holy Spirit.

Perhaps Dietrich Bonhoeffer was thinking of this type of frustrated layman when he pointed out:

> The man who fashions a visionary ideal of community demands that it be realized by God, by others, and by himself. He enters the community of Christians with his demands, sets up his own law, and judges the brethren and God Himself accordingly. He stands adamant, a living reproach to all others in the circle of brethren. He acts as if he is the creator of the Christian community, as if his dream binds men together. When things do not go his way, he calls the effort a failure. When his ideal picture is destroyed, he sees the community going to smash. So he becomes, first an accuser of his brethren, then an accuser of God, and finally the despairing accuser of himself.*

Now I don't mean to imply that no differences of opinion should exist in the Christian community. Quite the contrary. If the fellowship is enriched, as it should be, by a diversity of people, backgrounds, ideas, and opinions, real tensions will develop, heightened by the turmoil of a society undergoing radical change and the soul-searching of Christians groping for new value judgments amidst the turbulence. In fact, a church today which does not feel pressure and tensions is definitely not fulfilling God's purpose for its life in the world. It is at this point that congregations find themselves tested as never before. For only the presence of Christ at the center can quiet the bitter voice, reassure the anxious questioner, keep the faithful from faltering, unite otherwise dissident factions, and preserve the bonds of the Christian community.

In marked contrast to the sort of layman described by Bonhoeffer is the picture we get of John D. Rockefeller, Jr., the remarkable churchman who gave so generously of his wealth to New York City's Riverside Church. Of him, Harry Emerson Fosdick has written:

> One of the most considerate, friendly, self-effacing, co-operative persons I have ever known, he was so far from desiring to dominate either the church's policies or the minister's utterances that he has always leaned over backward to avoid

either. I have known him as a trustee of the Riverside Church to argue strongly against a proposed policy which the official boards were considering, and then when outvoted, I have seen him take the chairmanship of the committee appointed to put the policy into operation, and at the cost of hard work carry the matter he had voted against to a successful conclusion.*

Now on that positive note, Wayne, I shall end this letter. Christine just reminded me that we are due to leave within ten minutes for her college alumni society's annual banquet. I wasn't keen on attending this year, but when the matter was put to a vote, she exercised her wifely prerogative and decisively outvoted me. So, for the next few hours I shall join with many nice people at the festive board and try not to be a bore.

Faithfully,

Ken

"Let's Become Less Religious—and More Christian!"

Dear Wayne:

Apparently you found my description of a servant church appealing. You're beginning to see real merit in renewal. You even feel that you might accept this concept of Christianity without sacrificing your integrity. However, you raise a skeptical question which I must admit is both pragmatic and valid. What is gained by restructuring the church, you ask, only to have it perish in a storm of dissension and bitter acrimony?

But there *are* offsetting benefits emerging from this upheaval through which the church is going. There *are* significant gains which compensate for the noisy exodus of disgruntled church members fleeing liberal congregations.

First, there is an influx of new people joining creative congregations. The increase may be modest in size, but its potential is exciting. Some are transferring from ultraconservative churches after years of halfhearted affiliation. Others, who pulled out of "do-nothing" churches years ago, are now coming back to church but to a very different church! Still others never had an adult church affiliation. These are the people who during college discarded the superficial religion of their childhood and never replaced it with any viable substitute. Because they could not conscientiously dot the i's and cross the t's of conventional creeds, they considered themselves humanists, freethinkers, even atheists. Yet they sought to do

God's work in the secular city, often at the cost of spiritual loneliness and frustration.

In this latter group, Wayne, are many who have studied theology. My church's recent new-member training classes, for example, have included both graduates and dropouts from various theological seminaries. These new members had written off the church as an institutional heap of dry bones and turned to careers in other fields. Just think of all the fine young people the church has lost in recent years due to its rigidity, its unwillingness to sponsor creative experimentation, and its insistence that the parish minister become an organization man!

Second, these converts have been embracing today's "church creative" with almost missionary zeal. They are delighted to find here a freedom to study, to search, and to accept or reject in accordance with their consciences. In a word, they feel free to push ahead on their spiritual pilgrimage in the company of people who respect their integrity and offer them friendship and understanding. Unlike the typical Sunday morning pew warmers, these people eagerly involve themselves in the work of the church, tutoring potential high school dropouts, joining *koinonia* groups like the one which befriends patients recently discharged from a psychiatric hospital, working with teen-agers in our street ministry, or going down to our Covenant House to minister to the needs of people in an underprivileged neighborhood. Because the *living* church becomes so central to their life, these new members support it financially in a way that should shame many affluent members of long standing.

Third, we see creative churches drawing their members from an increasingly wider area. Like the Wesleys, who looked upon the world as their parish, the truly dynamic church today may have an entire metropolitan complex as *its* parish. Concerned Christians gladly drive past a score of staid churches in order to join a congregation that is earnestly on mission. They help to create a geographical, cultural, and economic fellowship that is representative of a cross section of society. I am thrilled, Wayne, when I see in our new-member training classes people from center city and from the suburbs; from Anglo-Saxon, Negro, and Oriental cultures; from prosperous homes and from tiny, often forlorn apartments; people who were educated in universities, and others who haltingly explain: "I can't talk so good, but I'm glad to be here, and hope maybe I can say something worth hearing." And they do, often with insights that enlarge our thinking and bring a twinge of shame to any who might initially have regarded them with a trace of condescension!

Fourth, the image of the church (to use an overworked term) undergoes gradual change. Community leaders involved in problems of public education, poverty, transportation, urban renewal, and other civic concerns initially view with skepticism the efforts of a church to relate to the community. They say, "Who are these dilettantes? Who are these do-gooders? They will learn soon enough that instead of finding glory and gratitude, they are likely to encounter only criticism, controversy, and power politics."

But if church people have the intestinal fortitude to stick with their mission, the community begins to accord the church a new respect. Before long, community meetings are being held in church buildings, and not in the town hall or the school auditorium. Moreover, church leaders begin to find that they can serve God better on a planning commission, a school board, a juvenile probation board, than on some church commission which makes mountains out of ecclesiastical molehills. Thus the truly creative church, called by God to be an agent of reconciliation, increasingly gets into the very thick of things where reconciliation is so urgently needed. This involvement is *not* at the expense of its life. Quite the contrary! By losing its old life of institutional concern about trivialities, the church now finds a new and exciting life based on concern for the welfare of God's people everywhere. Now the businessman, the scientist, the educator, and the artist begin to take the church seriously.

The fifth benefit is that the liberal attitude of creative churches today inevitably draws them together in mutual cooperation and concern without regard to denomination. In one sense, this might reflect a grim struggle for survival. But from a more constructive point of view, I believe it indicates a growing realization that *all* men—Protestant, Catholic, Jew, Buddhist, Mohammedan, Hindu—are seeking to find their proper relation to the God of all reality. And in this endeavor all men are brothers who can learn from one another, help one another, and through his grace make this world a more viable preparation for the next.

In my church this type of cooperation has been taking many forms. Roman Catholic prelates and choirs have participated in joint services in our sanctuary; and our ministers, choirs, and laymen have gone to many other churches and sectarian institutions. A Protestant-Catholic dialogue group was organized for biweekly worship, study, and the exchange of ideas. Several years ago a handful of ministers and lay people from six denominations came together informally to explore how people from different backgrounds might meet on neutral ground to discuss the problems of alienation which plague our metropolitan community and, hopefully, to find some basis for cooperative action. Thus was born "Wellsprings," an ecumenical renewal center which fosters dialogue between Christian and Jew, Catholic and Protestant, white man and black, urbanite and suburbanite. Today, Wellsprings has a paid staff of five people. They serve as codirectors, coordinator, and consultants. This staff is both interracial and interreligious, including Catholic, Protestant, and Jewish persons. At the Wellsprings Center, as well as in churches, synagogues, and schools throughout metropolitan Philadelphia, a variety of classes and seminars are held. As of this date, Wayne, more than five thousand people have attended Wellsprings "courses."

Wellsprings is building bridges between people who had never talked with one another previously. It is combating racial prejudice, anti-Semitism, and suburban sloth. It is often the scene of painful sessions, because the participants confront one another with honesty and candor instead of saying what the other person wants to hear. Through imaginative agencies like Wellsprings, the church creative is exercising new leadership in the battle for men's minds and allegiance at the point of need.

As a result of the tremendous upheaval of our society and the corresponding upheaval in the church, I believe I see the beginning of a significant metamorphosis. On one hand, some people pull out of a church which is agonizingly reappraising itself and striving to find a more relevant life. "This is not *my* church," they say. "Since I joined, you've changed all the rules. You're no longer religious." On the other hand, new people are coming into the church, exclaiming: "I never thought before there *could* be a church like this! This is what I've been looking for all my life. I want to get involved, challenged, committed!"

You see, here is the church changing from an institution in which the stress was on "being religious," where the emphasis was on the Sunday morning one-hour-a-week syndrome, and where professionally trained clergymen and missionaries were to save the world, and evolving instead into a church in which stress is on servanthood, a seven-day-a-week commitment, and a lay-oriented approach wherein *all* parishioners are members of the priesthood, to be on mission wherever they work or play.

In other words, Wayne, we now have a new and exciting option we may exercise, namely: "Let's become less religious—and more Christian!" Let's become more involved in the welfare of a brother and less concerned with glorifying the floodlit steeple. Let's be more concerned to do the work of the church and less tied down by "church-work." If we pursue these newer goals, I can see the Christian church evolving into smaller, leaner congregations which can accomplish greater things because the excess baggage that ties up our resources and manpower will be gone.

Of course, when I said "less religious," I exposed myself to misinterpretation. I did *not* mean to imply that we should worship God less. I was *not* agreeing with any theologian, seminarian, or minister who seems anxious to write off the church as an outmoded, vestigial throwback from an earlier period. Their attitude is that in this "post-Christian" era the church really doesn't serve much of a purpose, so let's cast it away. Let's free ourselves. Let's permit each Christian to serve his neighbor through community organizations, by working for social justice, by striving to improve the lot of the underprivileged, and by being just a good Christian humanist.

What these well-intentioned critics of the church blithely overlook is the essential importance of the community of believers to the practice and propagation of the faith. The Christian community is not an option, an appendage, an expendable adjunct, but it is the crucial center through which the Holy Spirit changes lives. To say that the community is not needed merely because often it has failed to live up to its God-given potential is to misunderstand the interdependent nature of worship and mission. We have found that receptivity to the Holy Spirit seems to be fostered by the alternate experience of life together in a vital worshiping community, and life apart as a member of that scattered brotherhood seeking to minister to the neighbor. When Bonhoeffer pointed out that a man can't be fit to live with others unless he becomes fit to live with himself, and *vice versa,* he seemed to be speaking also of the church. The congregation that finds its life in the mutually supportive roles of worship, prayer for one another, study, and fellowship must lose its life in loving service to others beyond its walls. But the congregation must return, again and again, for renewal of the Spirit and the support of the family in Christ. This dichotomy becomes imperative both for the church and for the individual. Without mission, worship degenerates into idolatry. And without worship, mission can become a hollow form of humanism.

Well, friend, how does all this strike you? Are you surprised—perhaps shocked—to hear me propose that we become less religious? Or does this please you because it indicates that our views about the church are not nearly as divergent as you had thought?

And how do you feel, Wayne, about the concept of Christian community as I have described it? Is this a kind of relationship which you, like most church members, never really have experienced? Is it something you crave perhaps subconsciously? Could it make a difference in your outlook on life?

I'd be interested, too, in your reaction to our need for worship vis-à-vis our need to serve our neighbor. Do you agree that they are mutually sustaining and that each validates and gives a new dimension to the other? Do you agree that Christianity is less a matter of comprehension (in the intellectual sense) than it is a matter of living for others (in the experiential sense of total participation)?

Austin Farrer expresses this totality of experience, and the way in which we and all men are a living part of God's continuing creation, when he observes:

> If we are concerned about a Creative Cause, it is because, in creating all things, he is creating us; and it concerns us to enter into the making of our souls, and of one another's. To enter into the action of God thus is what we mean by religion; and as it is something we do, it is a matter of experience.
>
> . . . by associating our wills with his [God's] working of them, we acquire experimental acquaintance with the work of God.
>
> . . . the embracing of God's will has the whole of a man's conduct for its outward expression. . . . God's will is my neighbour's good, and to see it I must look at my neighbour.*

After that, there is little left for me to say, except . . .

Bless you, neighbor!

Faithfully,

Ken

"It's Not the Coach Who Plays the Game!"

Dear Wayne:

I have just read your last letter, and it has given me what ad writers sometimes call a "satisfying, deep-down, good feeling." And do you know why? It's because we're really communicating with each other. The barriers between us have been lowered, perhaps more than you realize. I sense it in the directness of your remarks, the candor with which you disclose some of your innermost thoughts, and the interest you seem to be showing in certain aspects of personal renewal.

So you *haven't* really experienced a sense of community in your church! I'm not surprised. Few church members have. As you well express it, your congregation is like a group of commuters who see each other on the train but never really have the time to share one another's hopes and fears, triumphs and problems. Relationships are disturbingly shallow.

You also raise a pertinent question when you ask: "Is my minister really qualified, by temperament and training, to help to create the sense of community that you speak of? He's primarily a pulpit man, a dynamic preacher. Would he know how to go about forming one of those *koinonia* groups, as you call them?"

Wayne, perhaps I can suggest an answer by citing an anecdote. A few years ago the Right Reverend Leland Stark, Bishop of the Episcopal Diocese of Newark, N.J., was walking through a driving rain with a companion toward a lecture hall. On the way, the bishop was asked if he couldn't do something about the wretched weather. He replied: "No sir! I'm in sales, not management."

Ministers today, it seems to me, too often are rated for their sales promotional abilities. Pulpit committees travel about the country in search of spellbinders who can "sell" Christianity, almost as though the sins of the world could be washed away by some highly advertised brand of Christian detergent—preferably, one with a delightful scent capable of concealing any lingering odor of prejudice or bigotry. Indeed, if you survey the most highly paid ministers in America today, among them you are likely to find men with the gift of making the Christian religion as palatable, soporific, bland, and soothing as a big, sweet, sickening dose of paregoric. When you overhear such men chatting at a ministerial conference, it is difficult to distinguish them from a group of sales managers. Without losing his "cool," each one vies with his "competitors" in citing statistics on the size of congregations, gains in new members, increases in church budgets, and scope of current new building campaigns.

In this ecclesiastical rat race, the biggest and best numbers win. Obviously, the church of three thousand members *must* be more effective than a parish of only five hundred. A half-million dollar budget is not a sign of opulence but is proof that the work of Christ is getting done with efficiency and dispatch. One might be led to believe that the church is more anxious to extract dough from the oaf, than to be the leaven in the loaf!

I maintain that this professionalism of "selling" the gospel and glorifying numbers and size is nothing short of a perversion of the true gospel of Jesus Christ. It discredits the church and Christianity in the eyes of millions of people "on the outside." If we really are serious about our churchmanship as a means of proclaiming the good news of Christianity, we must recognize that only a small degree of the true ministry of the church can be performed by professionals. Instead, the entire priesthood of believers must be intent on serving their fellowmen in the spirit of Christ. Only through encounter with human need can the Christian find God in His deepest dimension.

Religion of this sort cannot be sold as a panacea to induce peace of mind or a sense of well-being. Quite the contrary. But what it *can* offer is a challenge to the faithful to respond to the call of a neighbor—to become involved in alleviating his suffering, to risk suspicion, ingratitude, even hostility, and to shoulder heavy responsibilities and thankless burdens, even the burden of a cross. Consequently, instead of evaluating the success of a parish on the basis of numbers, the true appraisal must be based on the *quality* of commitment of those who comprise the congregation.

Now anything as intangible as this is not very satisfying to the hierarchy of many denominations. It can't be neatly categorized on IBM cards or poured into statistical tables to impress those who pin their faith on reports. A ministerial friend of mine, recently returned from the slums of a Latin American city, was asked by his bishop: "How many decisions for Christ did you win during your month-long stay in South America, living with the people of an urban ghetto?" Having shared the almost unbelievable poverty, filth, and squalor of the peons, and having found it pathetically difficult to offer comfort to a people who already possessed an amazing trust in God despite their wretched condition, my friend could only exclaim to me, with tears in his eyes: "Statistics! Interested only in impressive figures, the damned fool!"

But to get back to our basic question, Wayne, just what type of minister do we need today? What qualifications equip him to organize a group of ordinary laymen into a powerful body of Christ? How can he avoid being submerged in an institutional bog of conferences, meetings, and reports? How can he free himself and his people from "church work" in order really to do the "work of the church"?

If we eliminate from consideration specialized types of ministries and focus on the needs of the parish church, it is my opinion that the attributes needed for a truly effective minister are radically different from the specifications drawn up by most pulpit committees.

First, the candidate qualified to fill today's needs must be a skilled and dedicated teacher, truly a "rabbi." Unless this man can help others to come to grips with the imperatives of the Bible and the teachings of Christ, and encourage them to acknowledge their uncertainties and perplexities, but at the same time inspire them to search for new and deeper meanings, he is not going to enable modern man to replace his adolescent church-school view of Christianity with a really mature faith capable of survival in our materialistic age.

Such a minister will be thoroughly familiar with enlightened interpretations of the Scriptures. He will understand the historical dimensions of the Old Testament and have a keen appreciation of our Judeo-Christian heritage, as well as the history of our church. He will know the chief theological channels through which Christian doctrines, both orthodox and liberal, have evolved. He will be familiar with other religions and their recorded teachings, such as the Vedas, the Koran, the Upanishads, the

Bhagavad-Gita, the Teachings of the Compassionate Buddha, and Lao-tzu's *Way of Life*. He will have read anthropology, psychology, sociology, and political science, realizing that only through understanding individual and group motivation can religious ideals be translated into secular action. He will be able to communicate effectively, not only from the pulpit but in small groups, where his familiarity with group dynamics will enable him to enlist the participation and the sharing of experiences by many diverse types of personalities. He will not have to know all the answers, Wayne! More important will be his ability to inspire confidence, display humility, and guide others in the search for the keys to the kingdom.

Second, I believe it imperative that he have adopted the discipline of a Christian style of life based upon daily study, Bible reading, and prayer (preferably with others). Without these resources, he may be intellectually equipped to comprehend the Christian gospel but emotionally unable to savor its mystery and excitement. A writer in *The Saturday Review* has expressed this extremely well by saying: "... the philosopher and the scientist endeavor to penetrate the Mystery, while the saint and the poet let themselves be penetrated by it." *

I am deeply disturbed that so many seminaries today seem to be producing graduates who are unable to open themselves to the power of the Holy Spirit. They appear to be getting a textbook-oriented academic training *about* faith without being exposed to those personal encounters in the world which develop, authenticate, and strengthen faith.

Let me cite an example of what I mean. Several years ago Bob Raines (Co-minister, First United Methodist Church of Germantown, Pa.) and I participated in a panel on the small-group type of ministry before the senior class of a large seminary. Bob spoke from the viewpoint of a minister, and I offered the viewpoint of a layman. Soon I got the impression that the seminarians didn't have much time for prayer because, to most of them, it appeared to be a superstitious form of exercise, like making a tape recording merely to train your voice, with the realization that no one but yourself ever will hear your words. When I spoke of the *koinonia* group of which I had been a member and the deep relationships which built up among those who began to live for one another, the seminarians asked unbelieving questions which indicated that they were accustomed to thinking on a more mundane and practical wavelength. Here are some of their refreshingly candid reactions (these were set down by one of their professors who monitored their "post mortem" after Bob and I had left):

Last Wednesday night the seniors met for an evangelism seminar and it was amazing how many seniors suddenly knew so much about the *koinonia* groups in which they had never been involved! This ignorance led to the discovery of all kinds of reasons why such groups are to be suspect: Mr. Raines' definition of love was not completely acceptable; and these groups could be labeled as experiments in amateur psychology. Well, let's get rid of our definitions if we think the Holy Spirit is bound by them. To label anything is an irresponsible way to dismiss a challenge. The point is, nothing will work if we start with the assumption that it won't and then act accordingly. This kind of assumption is found throughout the church today.

The honest thing to do would be: (a) Talk to men who have been involved in *koinonia* groups, whether their experience has been positive or negative. (b) The old cliche: pray about it. (c) Become involved in them yourself.

Many of us couldn't really understand Robert Raines and his associate because they spoke out of an experience that cannot be put into so many definitions. And I wager that if you become involved in such *koinonia* groups, you will have the same difficulty in explaining to others what has happened to you. You can't explain the work of the Holy Spirit.

Perhaps this is one reason why the doctrine of the Holy Spirit has been so neglected. One can easily state in intellectual terms an idea of God, and it is easy to describe the man Jesus Christ, because we too are men. But it is not easy to describe a Spirit that can only be encountered and experienced—and cannot be fully explained in black-and-white terms.

The key to Wednesday's discussion lies in the laymen present and in their understanding of the work of their respective churches. To single out the Methodist layman, how long has it been since you have seen one so enthusiastic about the work of his church? He spoke without hesitation about Jesus Christ and the work of the Holy Spirit in himself and his fellow Christians, of whatever race or background. Sunday morning is most often a fellowship of strangers, the opposite of the communion of saints. And "he who does not love his brother whom he has seen, cannot love God whom he has not seen" (1 John 4:20). The Holy Spirit knows where his church is, and it is not necessary for you and me to define the church down to the last statistic.

Actually an entire seminary, it seems to me, should be imbued with a desire to create among all its students a spiritual climate which fosters personal commitment. This requires a laboratory approach to education versus the more academic lecture method. That it is not looked upon with favor (except for periods of field work scheduled for most seminary middlers) may be seen in the difference between the academic status accorded professors who give such prestigious courses as Systematic Theology, Old Testament, New Testament, and Church History and professors who handle such utilitarian courses as Practical Theology or Pastoral Counseling. One hopeful note: a few seminaries are adding to their faculties laymen who are free of the academic compulsion to stress theology and who instead can delineate from firsthand experience some of the clergy-laity relationships which can often determine a young pastor's success or failure.

In this connection, layman William Stringfellow relates an amusing incident:

> I recall, for example, giving a lecture at a seminary a while ago in which I made a remark which particularly agitated the Dean of the seminary, and he said to me, "No responsible theologian would say what you just said!" That seemed to me reassuring news. A few days later I received a letter from someone who had been present at this exchange. The letter declared that the Dean had been mistaken and that in fact Soren Kierkegaard had written in his journals somewhere the substance of what I had said. I reported this comforting and distinguished citation to the Dean, who without hesitation announced: "Oh, Kierkegaard is not a responsible theologian." How could he be? He was no seminary professor. How could he know much about the mystery of God's presence in the world? Kierkegaard, after all, was only in the world—where God is—not in the seminary—where the theologians are! *

Third, a ministerial candidate should have a deep and abiding concern for people. He needs to see people as individual entities, as identifiable types in need of different forms of pastoral care—self-sufficient ones who need to be sensitized to their responsibility to others; shy persons with latent gifts who need the warm interest of another to help their budding talents develop; the handicapped persons, the emotionally disturbed, and the members of minority groups who have suffered indignities and thus should be the special concern of anyone who considers himself a Christian.

To meet such demanding requirements, the young pastor must be open and friendly, interested in listening attentively to people, able to distinguish real problems from the fancied plights of the neurotic, and alert to the danger signals which indicate the need for professional psychiatric help. He himself should have undergone sufficient screening to make certain that he is temperamentally equipped to be a shepherd of a flock. He must have the emotional maturity not to become involved with his parishioners in a way that will endanger his own health. In a word, he must possess firmness, but not hardness, of character. Sidney Smith gives us a clue to this important difference when he writes:

> Hardness of character is a want of minute attention to the feelings of others. It does not proceed from malignity or a carelessness of inflicting pain, but from a want of delicate perception of those little things by which pleasure is conferred or pain excited. *

Thus, with tact and warmth, the new minister draws together his people into an intimate Christian community. He guides them as they begin to share their lives together in study and prayer. Where this is done through the formation of *koinonia* groups (call them "re-search" groups, "study" groups, "Yokefellow" groups, or what you will), a bond develops which enables people to weather the storms of disagreement, controversy, or even dissension. As the people's understandings of stewardship grow, their financial giving increases. Seldom do they turn down responsible assignments. If the minister comes under fire, they are the first to spring to his defense. These people become true Christian ministers to one another, to the world, as represented by their neighbors, and— God be praised!—ministering to their minister. For to whom can *he* turn when he is troubled, discouraged, and uncertain of his next move? With whom can he seek counsel, knowing that his confidences will be respected? Not always to denominational leaders, for they often are too far removed from the actual scene to grasp the nuances of a parish problem involving personalities. It is in the *koinonia* group that the young minister finds resources of strength, understanding, and affection. From this kind of association comes one of the most rewarding experiences any young man can know.

This is what Paul really meant when he admonished the congregation at Ephesus:

> Therefore, putting away falsehood, let every one speak the truth with his neighbor, for we are members one of another. Be angry but do not sin; do not let the sun go down on your anger. . . . Let no evil talk come out of your mouths, but only such as is good for edifying, as fits the occasion, that it may impart grace to those who hear. . . . Let all bitterness and wrath and anger and clamor and slander be put away from you, with all malice, and be kind to one another, tenderhearted, forgiving one another, as God in Christ forgave you (Ephesians 4:25-26, 29, 31-32).

Fourth, our young minister should be able to shepherd his flock with prophetic vision. Now if you are about to protest that vision is only granted to the mature, experienced soul, I must disagree. This is not something a man acquires by trying harder; vision is a "given" thing— an exciting, often mystical, merging of a sensitive spirit, a creative imagination, and a quiet confidence that history can be shaped by opening ourselves to God's will. I have known some remarkable young men who after looking at people and at society, have been able to discern ways of closing gaps between God's imperatives and man's selfish resistance to change.

These four attributes, it seems to me, provide a vital center around which a dynamic Christian community can be formed.

But you ask, Wayne, how the many ministries needed by a typical parish are going to get done if our pastor is tied up with following his disciplined style of life, with leading public worship, with training, educating, and inspiring the members of his parish! Who is going to handle the evangelism of the church? Who is going to call on prospective new members? Who is going to visit the sick in hospitals and nursing homes? Who is going to give the invocation at meetings of the Rotary Club, the Chamber of Commerce, or the Lions Club? Who is going to assist in the service of worship by reading the Scriptures, offering the pastoral prayer, even conducting the service itself? If the minister becomes sick, who is going to preach the sermon? If a retreat is to be held for groups from the church, who is to provide leadership? If other churches ask for speakers, or help in organizing *koinonia* groups, or someone to inspire their laity with a vision of the potential which lies within their grasp, who is to answer the call?

To all of these questions, there is just one answer: the laity! In a parish which comprises committed lay people, they will be doing these things, and more. For this is *their* church. *They* are the members of the body of Christ. Ours is a do-it-yourself religion, in which we all are true ministers.

Of course at times of crisis, such as critical illness, and death and bereavement, the professional minister is indispensable. He brings to the need an expertise which is essential. But in most other areas of life, the layman goes where the ordained minister cannot go: in the daily work situation in office, store, or factory; in the schoolroom; in the offices of government, trade association, union, and fraternal groups. In these worldly meeting places the layman becomes the leaven in the loaf, the candle lit in a dark world, the indwelling presence of Christ in our very midst. And because the layman is not a "pro," and takes positions on controversial subjects without any motivation other than a personal concern, his words and actions can make a strong impact on those who customarily look for an angle based on selfish gain.

At the point of equipping the laity for their mission in the world, many liberal clergymen fail to understand their role. Today's men of the cloth too often think they are going to remake society single-handedly. By getting on a picket line, participating in a demonstration, or appearing at meetings on social issues, a minister is perhaps filling some inner urge for personal involvement. On some occasions this action may be called for, but the *real* decisions are made at points of power in executive suites, political caucuses, committee meetings, court chambers, and union halls. These constitute the playing field where the team of laymen gets involved in the game of life. If the coach has done his job, the members of the team will know their roles. They may even look to the bench for guidance. But the point which needs stressing is this: a good coach does not develop himself as a player, but he develops a whole team of players! He drills them on the fundamentals of the game. He helps plot the strategy. If he attracts good material to his squad, his team becomes adept at responding to unexpected challenges, like grabbing the ball and running with it.

So let's remember, Wayne, it's not the coach who plays the game!

But let's remember, too, that throughout the game each player must be aware of the referee, who has laid down certain guidelines. The game simply must be played according to His rules, else sooner or later the entire team will be penalized. Furthermore, a coach is judged by the performance of his team, not by his own personal brilliance.

Just think of the dynamic power of a church of five hundred members in which every member is an actual minister! And think of the power of Christianity in our nation if all of the millions of church members could be truly committed Christians, on mission every day of the week!

Does all this seem visionary? Does it sound as though I have been talking about something that is impossible? Well, it *can* be achieved! For I have been privileged to serve in a church community where hundreds of people have become involved in trying to make their religion a central force in their daily lives. And I can assure you that this kind of commitment has changed my life in many radical ways and has given me a joy never before experienced.

But more of this in another letter. In the meantime, my warm regards!

Faithfully,

Ken

"Don't Wait for the Reader's Digest!"

Dear Wayne:

You're right. The specifications in my last letter for a parish minister are stiff. To meet them he must be an exceptional young man. But then, why shouldn't he be? For many years our outstanding college graduates chose careers in business, medicine, engineering, or law. These fields offered high financial rewards and status. Many thought of the ministry as a third or fourth choice. I recall hearing a young man actually say: "Well, there's one thing about the ministry; you always have a job. It's safe, and you don't have to work too hard!"

What an attitude to have about one of the most demanding, most exhausting, most rewarding of professions!

But today we are seeing a different spirit in many young people. There has been a marked change for the better in their value judgments. The unprecedented prosperity of the past two decades has diminished the incentive for making a fortune which motivated the youth of our generation. Most people have incomes that are at least adequate for their basic needs. Now the kids are looking critically at this world of ours and vowing that they want to do something about correcting its glaring inequities. As a result, we find more and more idealism. There is more and more interest in careers that will be intellectually, emotionally, and spiritually satisfying.

Wayne, you are right in pointing out that if a minister's job is exciting and rewarding, it also can be precarious. A friend of mine who counsels with ministers throughout a four-state area for his denomination tells me that fully 80 percent of those he talks with would leave their churches tomorrow *if* they had any assurance that another church would not confront them with even more vexing problems.

In your last letter you mentioned that members of your congregation have been criticizing your newest minister because he sports a beard. Reactions of this type to the personal whims of clerics are commonplace in the United States, with its Puritan heritage. Recently a member of our own church said to me: "I hope I'm not old-fashioned, but somehow I want my minister to be a better man than I am. I want to feel that I can look up to him and respect him for his way of life."

"Do you expect your broker, your banker, your physician, or your attorney to be a better man than you are in order to win your respect?" I asked. "Or do you insist, instead, that he know infinitely more about his specialty than you do—in other words, that he be an authority in his field, well qualified to advise and counsel you?"

"But that's different," he countered. "Somehow, I expect my spiritual adviser to practice what he preaches. I want to admire him."

"You want him to be a saint?" I asked.

My friend hesitated a bit. "W-e-l-l, perhaps not a saint, but at least a very religious person."

This man was expressing a widely held misconception regarding the clergy. What he was really saying is: "I don't want to change my life in any radical way simply because I am a member of a church. I don't want Jesus Christ really to transform my life. That would require me to make all sorts of sacrifices, changes in my value judgments, and even accept a discipline or style of life. What I want, instead, is my minister to become my representative, my proxy. I want him to live out the sort of life that Christ asks *me* to live out. In this way, Christianity will not disturb me personally. It will not require me to deny myself, which is certainly one thing I don't want to do in this day of indulgence. In effect, then, my minister can be the expiation for my sins." This attitude is, of course, a popular perversion of the entire concept of the Protestant faith, which holds that it was Jesus Christ who, through his sacrifice, absolved us of our guilt.

Speaking of more personal matters, Wayne, it was great being with you and Margaret last Friday at Joan's wedding. The bride looked as sweet and pure as brides are supposed to be. The groom looked worried enough to convince the maiden ladies present that he was contemplating his wedding night without benefit of rehearsals as thorough as had been staged for the ceremony itself. The bridesmaids fluttered their eyelashes demurely as they minced their way down the aisle, and the ushers seemed to have just the right blend of dignity and boredom.

Did you know that all the ushers were seminarians, classmates of the groom? That's why it startled me when I heard that the groom's wedding gift to each of his ushers, and to his best man, was a hip flask. A rebellious gesture, perhaps, to show the world that today's seminarian is at least as worldly-wise as the man in the pew.

But my greatest surprise came during the reception while you, Margaret, Christine, and I were sitting at the table enjoying the excellent refreshments provided by Joan's family. Your remark about the minister who officiated at the ceremony really startled me. Apparently he made a deep impression upon you. Seldom have I heard you be quite as complimentary about the way a clergyman, especially one from a "conventional" denomination, has conducted a service. Inwardly I asked myself, "Just what was there about this man's rather mundane manner which so moved you? Whatever did he say or do that penetrated your armor of sophistication? Not his voice, for it was somewhat bland and colorless. Not his personality, for his handling of the service, although adequate, was not inspiring."

But while I was fruitlessly searching my memory, you suddenly broke the mystery wide open by exclaiming: "Boy, that stuff he said about love was simply beautiful! I have never heard anyone express so well what I have felt to be true but could never put into words. How it makes you realize your shortcomings! So many of his words applied to me. And what terrific advice for a bride and groom! What a minister!"

Far from extemporizing, the clergyman had been reading Paul's immortal words from the thirteenth chapter of First Corinthians:

Love is patient and kind; love is not jealous or boastful; it is not arrogant or rude. Love does not insist on its own way; it is not irritable or resentful; it does not rejoice at wrong, but rejoices in the right. Love bears all things, believes all things, hopes all things, endures all things (1 Corinthians 13:4-7).

You see how the Word of God can travel straight to a man's heart, Wayne, when it relates to some situation in our daily life. Then God's word is powerful and relevant!

I guess the real shock to me, though, was that these beautifully expressed truths were so unfamiliar to you. I shouldn't have been surprised, for in this day and age the average church member simply is not familiar with his Bible. I recall the question which Christine recently overheard a woman asking her pastor: "Could you tell me in what part of the Bible I can find the famous prayer of St. Francis of Assisi?" This question understandably shook up the good cleric. To his slightly bewildered parishioner he gently explained that the good saint did his writing more than a thousand years after the New Testament was completed.

Because I mention these things, Wayne, don't think I am being condescending. I'm not trying to ridicule others or sit in judgment over them. Far from it. Not until eight or ten years ago did I begin to read the Bible with any degree of regularity. Prior to that I had a vague sort of curiosity about it and a desire to explore its mysteries. But the sheer size of the Bible makes this a formidable undertaking, especially in this age of terse, telegraphic communication. Like many other people, I was probably waiting to see if the *Reader's Digest* would bring it out in condensed form.

May I offer a bit of friendly advice? Don't wait for the *Reader's Digest!*

Let me say, emphatically, that no one can consider himself an informed Christian unless he has a basic knowledge of the Bible and sufficient familiarity with its structure to be able to find in it pertinent material as needed. I don't say this in any spirit of bibliolatry, for I have no sympathy with those who substitute Bible quoting for ministering to those in need. But if it seems unreasonable to insist upon this sort of background as a prerequisite, just ask yourself how any law student could become much of a lawyer without a knowledge of Blackstone. How could a medical student become much of a physician without intimate knowledge of Gray's *Anatomy,* supplemented, of course, by the experience of dissecting a cadaver?

Becoming familiar with the Bible raises a practical question: How does a person in this busy world, with all of its time-consuming responsibilities and distractions, go about acquiring an understanding of so extensive a compilation of history, philosophy, and wisdom? Can it be done by starting at the beginning and plowing through the many books of the Old and the New Testaments?

One of my friends tried this but found the going tough. "I started with Genesis," he reported, "and after completing the Garden of Eden epic, I waded straight through the chronology of all those people who spent their leisure time begetting offspring—that is, when they weren't indulging in incest, fornication, and other forms of extracurricular activity. I must say it unnerved me to realize that my distant ancestors were such a crummy lot. After a week of this, I hadn't even finished Genesis.

I simply gave up. You might say that I made my personal exodus before I even reached the Exodus of the tribes of Israel!"

Actually my friend approached his project with such grim determination that he overlooked all the fun and excitement. Unless a person is inordinately interested in history, he might better start his reading in the New Testament, where situations and Christian philosophy relate more directly to our daily living. However, if the Old Testament has a fascination for him, he could begin reading the insights of prophets like Isaiah, Jeremiah, or Ezekiel.

Apart from the content itself, if a study of the Bible is to be fruitful, it must be approached in a thoughtful, reflective frame of mind. Only in this way can the priceless truths locked within the words, phrases, figures of speech, and parables really be found to have relevance to the situations we face in the twentieth century. Approached in this spirit, the Bible becomes as current as today's newspaper, in spite of the vastly different economic and cultural setting in which it is laid.

Would you be willing, Wayne, to expose yourself to the potential power which can be released by serious Bible study? If so, I suggest that you begin with one of Paul's magnificent letters to the early churches of his day. Try Ephesians, perhaps, or Philippians, or Romans. In view of how moved you were by the reading from First Corinthians at the wedding service, you might find any of these letters absorbing and rewarding.

Next, equip yourself with a good commentary. It could be a volume from the famous *Interpreter's Bible,* or a commentary by someone like Barclay. In either case, I suggest two basic techniques which should help you to derive the most from the time you spend.

First, don't make the common mistake of trying to read an inordinately long passage at one sitting. It is much better to take only one chapter, or only a portion of a chapter, unless, of course, you are reading a chronicle of events. If the passage deals with philosophic or ethical matters keep it short.

Second, it is vitally important to read the passage at least once, and preferably many times, each day for a period of, say, two weeks. You ask: "Why all this repetition? Surely it would seem more rewarding to read a new chapter each day."

My reply simply is this: Most biblical passages are packed with significance and insight. Seldom are the great truths on the surface. Because human nature, regrettably, has not changed significantly in the last few thousand years, the relations between individuals and their relations with God still involve essentially the same human struggle between fear and hope, selfishness and magnanimity, greed and generosity, and cruelty and compassion. Only the economic order, the level of technology, the socio-political milieu have changed. But what crucial changes these are! For by becoming increasingly sophisticated, we've reached the point where an immoral action can affect not merely hundreds of innocent victims, but millions. In other words, we have succeeded in amplifying the *consequences* of man's basic decisions, but we have not succeeded in improving the *quality* of those decisions. Thus our potential for good or evil has become frightening in its implications.

Therefore, two different frames of reference must be applied to Bible reading. First, we must visualize the conditions which existed at the time the chronicle was recorded. Only in this way can we comprehend what questions of that day were being answered in a particular passage. Second, we must read the same passages in the light of conditions today, asking what relevance the eternal truths of the Bible hold for us. Only by these techniques can God's light clarify our problems.

Wayne, this letter has grown to be so long that you might accuse me of writing an epistle. Unless, of course, you walked out on me several pages back to read *Look* or *Life*. But if you'll permit a pun this late in the evening, you can get a better look at life from the perspective of the Bible.

Honest!

Faithfully,

Ken

"From 2000 Light-Years the View Becomes Clearer!"

Dear Wayne:

You *are* a good sport! I'm grateful to you for acknowledging that if the New Testament has many other passages as good as the First Corinthians essay on love, it deserves to be called "The Good Book."

I'm sorry you're so upset about my proposal for repeated readings of the same passage. "What is accomplished by this sort of exercise?" you demand. "Do you advocate the committing of verses to memory? Do you want people to rattle them off and then, with a superior smirk, say: 'John 3:16'?"

No, Wayne, I do not. Believe me, there *is* a rationale to what I'm suggesting, and it's simply this: By reading the same passage day after day, you actually will begin to "live under the Word." That's a rather high-flown way of saying that as you encounter new situations, you will find guidance for your life from truths which have their roots in man's history and God's revelation. The Bible, you see, links us with the past *and* with the future. In that sense it is timeless. That's why I believe you'll be amazed to find how many new meanings and fresh insights can rise to the surface only after you've read a passage for the sixth or seventh time. This may happen simply because events that occur in your daily living give particular relevancy often to words and phrases which formerly remained meaningless.

Let's take a concrete example. Let's assume that we are reading the book of Acts. This book opens, in point of time, immediately following Christ's resurrection and his appearance to the apostles. As we read, we gain an exciting picture of the birth of the church as seen in the coming of the Holy Spirit at Pentecost, the baptizing of the initial thousands who joined the new fellowship, the increasing antagonism of the priests who feared that this new religion would undermine their authority and status, the widespread persecution of the early Christians, and the gradual spreading of the faith among the Gentiles of nearby countries in the Mediterranean world.

Let's assume further that we recently read of the stoning of Stephen by the mob which became aroused as they heard him indict the slayers of Jesus for their ruthless crime. "Lord Jesus, receive my spirit," cried out Stephen as he was battered by a barrage of stones. And then, as Saul of Tarsus watched from the edge of the mob, Stephen knelt and cried out with a loud voice, "Lord, do not hold this sin against them."

With this background, Wayne, we now turn to the ninth chapter, a passage telling of Saul's amazing conversion from a persecutor of Christians to one who propagated Christianity with missionary zeal:

But Saul, still breathing threats and murder against the disciples of the Lord, went to the high priest and asked him for letters to the synagogues at Damascus, so that if he found any belonging to the Way, men or women, he might bring them bound to Jerusalem. Now as he journeyed he approached Damascus, and suddenly a light from heaven flashed about him. And he fell to the ground and heard a voice saying to him, "Saul, Saul, why do you persecute me?" And he said, "Who are you, Lord?" And he said, "I am Jesus, whom you are persecuting; but rise and enter the city, and you will be told what you are to do." The men who were traveling with him stood speechless, hearing the voice but seeing no one. Saul arose from the ground; and when his eyes were opened, he could see nothing; so they led him by the hand and brought him into Damascus. And for three days he was without sight, and neither ate nor drank.

Now there was a disciple at Damascus named Ananias. The Lord said to him in a vision, "Ananias." And he said, "Here I am, Lord." And the Lord said to him, "Rise and go to the street called Straight, and inquire in the house of Judas for a man of Tarsus named Saul; for behold, he is praying, and he has seen a man named Ananias come in and lay his hands on him so that he might regain his sight." But Ananias answered, "Lord, I have heard from many about this man, how much evil he has done to thy saints at Jerusalem; and here he has authority from the chief priests to bind all who call upon thy name." But the Lord said to him, "Go, for he is a chosen instrument of mine to carry my name before the Gentiles and kings and the sons of Israel; for I will show him how much he must suffer for the sake of my name." So Ananias departed and entered the house. And laying his hands on him he said, "Brother Saul, the Lord Jesus who appeared to you on the road by which you came, has sent me that you may regain your sight and be filled with the Holy Spirit." And immediately something like scales fell from his eyes and he regained his sight. Then he rose and was baptized, and took food and was strengthened.

To illustrate how the daily rereading of such a passage might deepen our understanding of it, Wayne, I'm going to set down in diary form the reactions which might arise in a reader's mind. As you read these imagined notes, please don't be too critical; just relax and see if the cumulative effect doesn't lead you to a deeper insight. Here we go!

Monday: I read the assignment today for the first time. What a story! The flash of light and the voice from heaven sound like a miracle of some kind. So does the sudden blindness and the regaining of sight three days later. I find it hard to buy such superstitious stuff.

Tuesday: I was reading the verses from Acts this evening on the train when Bill Landis dropped into the seat beside me. Haven't seen Bill for weeks. I tried to conceal the pocket-size New Testament, but Bill saw it and wanted to know what I was reading. I felt silly about telling him, afraid he'd think I was becoming a religious nut. He didn't scoff but said something about wishing some of his patients at the psychiatric clinic could get some faith in God, or in him, or in somebody. I asked him about the flash of light and the blindness. Was such a thing possible, psychologically? He said that he had known a case or two where a tremendous shock had induced an hysterical sort of blindness. Lasted a week or two, in one instance. So something like that *could* happen.

Wednesday: According to a commentary on Acts, Saul was a very religious character. A Jew who always observed the law. An aggressive guy who wanted to get ahead. Bet he was emotional! The way he went about persecuting the Christians indicated that. Imagine a chap going to the high priests and asking for what amounted to a hunting license authorizing him to seize any male or female Christians he could find and bring them back in shackles to Jerusalem! He must really have been caught up in the "hate Christians" hysteria. Like some extremists today hate Jews or Negroes.

Thursday: After reading the passage again I got to wondering if Saul had been storing up a lot of guilt over his persecution of the Christians. If he had, it could set the stage for a tremendous emotional experience. That could account for his experience on the road to Damascus. But what might have triggered it? I went back to the end of Chapter 7 and reread the bit about the stoning of Stephen. I was then struck by a similarity between Stephen's death and Christ's. At one point during his crucifixion Jesus said, "Father, into thy hands I commit my spirit," and Stephen, undoubtedly thinking of Christ during his last moments of life, is quoted as saying, "Lord Jesus, receive my spirit." In addition, Jesus said, "Father, forgive them; for they know not what they do," and similarly Stephen cried with a loud voice, "Lord, do not hold this sin against them."

Saul must have known a lot about Jesus. When he watched the stoning of Stephen, he may have felt as if he were seeing the Crucifixion re-enacted. Yet he did nothing. Just stood there in silence. Maybe he was reluctant to get involved, like some people are today. What a lot of guilt he must have been accumulating!

Friday: Had a phone call this evening from our minister. He wanted me to call on Ben and Muriel White. Seems that they've gotten teed off on the race issue, especially since the Johnsons, that black family down on Elm Street, joined our church. I told Mr. Littleton I'd like to help, but that Ben just happens to be one of my customers and I wouldn't want to antagonize him; he represents a very profitable account. Mr. Littleton seemed a bit disappointed, but he's a good sport. Said maybe he'd ask someone else.

Saturday: Had to go to the office today to sign out several bid proposals which Marjorie finished typing Friday night. On the train I read the Acts passage again. Golly, I'm almost getting to know it by heart! I was intrigued that the Lord asked Ananias to go to Saul, instead of completing the job himself. That seemed strange. To ask an ordinary guy like Ananias —a layman—to help finish what he started with that flash and thunder bit on the road to Damascus seemed very strange. But then I reread what Ananias said: "Lord, I have heard from many about this man, how much evil he has done to thy saints at Jerusalem." It dawned on me that this layman felt real apprehension about going to Saul. God was asking him to risk his neck. Then my telephone conversation with Mr. Littleton hit me like a ton of bricks! I had been in a position a little like Ananias. But I was afraid to risk *my* neck because Ben might resent me and take away his profitable business. Golly, did I feel cheap, almost remorseful! As soon as I got to the office, I phoned the parson. Told him I'd be glad to make the call, that is, if he hadn't already asked someone else. I was astounded by his reply: "No, I haven't. Somehow, I had faith you might be led to reconsider." How thankful I am that I did! Too, I've found another hint for me in that passage from Acts. When Ananias went to Saul, he laid his hands on him and called him "Brother Saul." Imagine calling a guy who had been persecuting your own friends "Brother"! I must admit that ever since Mr. Littleton first phoned me about calling on Ben and Muriel, I felt a chip on my shoulder toward

Ben. I kind of resented the way he feels toward that black family in our church. But now I realize this is wrong. I shouldn't pass judgment on him. It's my job to go in a spirit of friendship, or I'd better not go at all.

Sunday: Joe Littleton had a darned good sermon today. He spoke about different forms of conversion and how frustrated some people feel because they never had a spectacular experience. But he pointed out that conversion often takes the form of a quiet, powerful realization of the authenticity of Christ; indeed he is the truth, the way, and nothing else is needed; nothing else matters. Although I was listening intently to the sermon, I was also thinking about Ben, the call I'll be making on him, and that I may be the layman whom God has chosen to reconcile Ben and our black friends. Kind of scary thought, too, until I realized that it will have to be *God* who does the job through me. Thank you, God, for that reminder! And I found myself thinking of Saul and how that great flash of truth about Christ must have hit him! Poor guy! Little wonder he couldn't see for three days. But the question that has been bugging me about exactly what *did* happen on the road to Damascus—whether it was a miracle, an illusion, or some form of hysteria—just doesn't seem very important now. The significant point is that it happened. The radical change in Paul's life certainly proves this beyond a doubt. Oh, yes, in his sermon Mr. Littleton used the word "mystery" quite often, too. That word used to bother me. It sounded like the old "cover-up" for things we can't explain. But that doesn't trouble me any more, either. I guess if I could understand the force behind these things, I wouldn't be a mere man. I'd be God!

And there we have it, Wayne.

Remember the first astronauts who encircled the moon and viewed our earth from a distance of 232,000 miles? Do you recall with what poignant emotion they gazed upon our richly endowed planet, aware as never before of man's failure to make it the kind of bountiful dwelling place it should be?

Well, the reading of the Bible can perform something of the same service for us. In space-age terms: "From 2000 light-years the view becomes clearer!" Clearer, because the transient turmoil of the moment recedes into its proper place. Clearer, because the eternal truths tested by the years come strongly into focus. In short, we are enabled to view our situation a bit more from God's perspective instead of entirely from our own.

This idea leads me to a few final points before I close this letter and tumble into bed. First, don't fall into the trap of trying to take all the miracles of the Bible literally. Many people do. Either they blindly accept the entire collection as "gospel truth," which is a stiff challenge to a thinking person's credulity, or they get frustrated and shrug off the entire lot as silly fantasy. Bultmann has done us a great disservice by his crusade-like efforts to demythologize the Bible. Actually, the learned men of biblical times were not fools; they didn't fall for old wives' tales and parade them before us as fact. But they *were* poets, in the sense that they expressed intangible, difficult-to-grasp concepts in terms of allegory, metaphor, and symbolism so that mere man could comprehend them. As we know, Jesus himself used countless parables to illustrate his teachings. Certainly to be avoided, Wayne, is engaging in fruitless argument about the validity of the *form* in which a truth is couched and thereby missing its *substance*.

Second, avoid turning to the Bible in search of support for a particular favorite point of view. Many people do this. I call them "Bible lawyers." Like an attorney hunting for citations to use in the defense of a client, they avidly scan page after page to find some quotation which they can lift out of context to prove that God is on their side. Actually, we should turn to the Bible with open mind and heart to hear what God seeks to say to us. We may not like what we find, for biblical writers had a habit of pointing their fingers at human weakness. Remember, Wayne, how moved you were by Paul's definition of unselfish *agape* love when the minister read it at the wedding? That's how the Bible should speak to us. And if the Revised Standard Version seems obscure at some point, turn to the King James version, or the Phillips translation, or the *New English Bible,* or the Anchor version. Find the phraseology that conveys meaning to *you.* Nevertheless, be sure you're listening to God's word and not to your own self-justification.

Third, although Bible study is possible on a solo basis, it is the hard way to do it. There is the difficulty of adhering to a study schedule besides the disadvantage of losing other points of view. That is why I strongly urge membership in a *koinonia* group. By meeting regularly with others of similar aim, you gain impetus, encouragement, and a fellowship in Christ which can enrich your pilgrimage. For *koinonia* is not only study together; it encompasses prayer, sharing, concern for others, and all such aspects of community which the Christian church is supposed to provide, but so rarely does.

Robert Raines summarizes it succinctly out of his extensive experience with the small-group ministry when he says:

There cannot be real firsthand *koinonia* among hundreds of people. The best evidence of this is the fact that hundreds of people in a given local church can worship faithfully for years without any appreciable change in quality of commitment or direction of life. Many of the same people, exposed to a breath or taste of *koinonia* in some small group, begin to change in a matter of months. The church is obligated to lead its people into small-group fellowship where the conditions for *koinonia* prevail.*

So, Wayne, I covet this kind of experience for you. It could change your entire outlook on life. It changed mine.

Faithfully,

Ken

"Come as You Are!"

Dear Wayne:

Glad to hear that you've talked with your minister about forming a *koinonia* group. Now, because the idea is new in your church, you are asking for some pointers.

This is wonderful news! I'm delighted that you and Margaret are willing to join such a group and to explore the exciting possibilities in it for growth in faith and understanding. Without wishing to overstate the case, I honestly believe you may find this to be a significant step in your quest for deeper meaning in life. Dialogue stimulates and challenges, exposes us to new points of view, forces us to reexamine our prejudices, helps us to rethink our goals, and provides a welcome contrast to the monologue which in many churches promotes passive pew-sitting and escape from involvement.

Now let us deal with your specific questions: How do you structure a *koinonia* group? Do you seek to bring together congenial people? If so, how do you deal with those who may want "in," but simply won't fit?

May I suggest that you and your minister first list the members of your congregation who you feel might be interested in *koinonia*. Use great care in making up this list. Don't include people from just one stratum in your church, simply because they might say "yes." Ideally, the group should be composed of those of a diversity of backgrounds, ethnic origins (if possible), and economic levels. If, instead, you bring together a homogeneous coterie of people, you will defeat the deeper purposes of *koinonia.* As you know, most "secular" groups are formed around some strong central interest as, for example, music, contract bridge, ice skating, or the breeding of dogs.

But the motivation of a *koinonia* group should be entirely different. Here the concern of all is with Christ. He becomes the center, the focus, the single uncommon denominator. He is the catalyst who inspires dissimilar people to seek his will for their lives by forming a Christian community, in which members of the "family" learn to open their lives to each other through the sharing of study, prayer, and mutual concern.

Dietrich Bonhoeffer has emphasized:

> Every principle of selection and every separation connected with it that is not necessitated quite objectively by common work, local conditions, or family connections is of the greatest danger to a Christian community. When the way of intellectual or spiritual selection is taken the human element always insinuates itself and robs the fellowship of its spiritual power and effectiveness for the Church, drives it into sectarianism. The exclusion of the weak and insignificant, the seemingly useless people, from a Christian community may actually mean the exclusion of Christ; in the poor brother Christ is knocking at the door. We must, therefore, be very careful at this point.*

Another question! You have a fear, Wayne, that people may shy away from coming into the group because they would feel embarrassed to pull out if it failed to measure up to their expectations. A good point! But it is easy to deal with.

After the list is made up, you and your minister should decide on a specific trial period. Twelve weeks would make a good term. With meetings normally held at two-week intervals in the homes of members on a rotating basis, this will provide six trial sessions. By thus limiting the initial period, no participant commits himself indefinitely. This is important. Not only will more invitees accept your invitation, but at the end of the period the group can assess the value of the meetings and decide upon their future course. Here is a healthy, democratic procedure.

Incidentally, just last evening I had a telephone call from the lay leader of the Catholics who participated in our first Catholic-Protestant dialogue group. She is a woman skilled in group dynamics. The group had completed its tentative trial run of six meetings. The question had been raised: "In view of all the Catholics and Protestants in our respective parishes who would like to engage in dialogue, is the group willing to be divided into two 'seed' groups, each taking in enough new people to make each group consist of fifteen members?" I was delighted, at this stage of their development, to hear their answer: "No, we don't want to be separated. We are having a great experience of sharing and getting to understand one another. We want this to continue, without dilution, so our relationship can begin to deepen."

But to continue with your questions: "In forming a *koinonia* group, how do you avoid creating a group consisting only of 'in' people, a situation deeply resented by others in the church?"

A good precaution, Wayne. Your next step should be to send your prospects a special letter, signed by your minister and, preferably, also by you, inviting them to the minister's home on a specified night to discuss membership in such a group. Some of these people should also be contacted more personally. Concurrently, it is important to issue a church-wide invitation through your church bulletin or newsletter. This will avoid what you fear—any implication that this *koinonia* idea is exclusive and only for a favored few. Be prepared, however, for a response which may require the initial formation of more than one group. When we first launched a *koinonia* program in our church some years ago, fifty-five people came to the minister's home for our exploratory meeting, and of these some forty-five decided to take part in a "trial run." This necessitated the formation of three groups, for experience has shown that fifteen people comprise an optimum number. If there are fewer than ten persons, the group lacks sufficient breadth and diversity of background for rewarding discussion. More than fifteen, on the other hand, can inhibit participation by the more timid.

Another question: "How do you handle the idly curious who might come to only a meeting or two?"

At the exploratory session, Wayne, invite someone experienced with *koinonia*-type groups. Such a person can be of considerable assistance in explaining the philosophy and objectives of *koinonia* and the structure of the meetings. Emphasize at the outset that all who choose to participate in the "trial run" must agree to four important priorities.

First, attendance at every *koinonia* meeting will be obligatory, except in cases of illness or absence from town. Second, each person must agree to read the assigned material thoughtfully and reflectively. Biblical passages of short or moderate length are to be read daily. Third, each person must agree to pray daily for the needs and concerns of others in the group. Such prayer is not only intercessory on behalf of the person prayed for, but by defining the need, the person who is praying is asking how to minister to that need. Fourth, each person must seek to become increasingly sensitive to the talents and resources of the group and the way those resources might be used for some collective form of mission.

You see, Wayne, if anyone doesn't intend to take *koinonia* seriously, he should eliminate himself at the very outset.

Certain additional matters will require attention at this initial meeting. There is the choice of a study topic—something that will cover the span of six meetings satisfactorily. Although this can be some current book dealing with applied Christianity (*The Creative Years* by Reuel Howe, for example, or *The Meaning of Persons* by Paul Tournier), I strongly recommend that the initial meetings be based on a book of the Bible. Epistles like Ephesians, Philippians or Colossians are well suited to the allotted span of time.

Also there is the question of leadership, and this should be evaluated by you and your minister just as soon as you know who will be participating. Usually the minister himself should be present, not necessarily as the discussion leader, but as a resource person to whom questions of a more scholarly nature can be referred. The time will come when leadership within the group develops to a point where the minister can drop out, returning from time to time simply to check on the group's progress or in response to a call for expert guidance. Incidentally, the discussion leadership may be assumed by one outstandingly qualified person, or it may rotate among members of the group.

And now to answer your question about the structure of a typical meeting!

Let's assume that the topic, the study material, and the discussion leader have been chosen. The meeting will be held in the home of one of the members, who also has consented to lead the devotions. It has been agreed that meetings will start at eight o'clock and terminate at nine forty-five for refreshments, during which private discussions can continue for as long as people may desire. Furthermore, refreshments will be limited to tea, coffee, and cookies. There must be nothing more elaborate, so that there will be no basis for competition by subsequent hostesses.

As soon as all participants have arrived, the leader of devotions suggests a period of silence. This permits what our Quaker friends call "centering down." It brings the relaxing of tensions at the close of the day and the quieting of the mind so that, hopefully, we may be receptive to one another and to the presence of the Spirit. Initially, the quiet period may last only a minute or two. Later, as the group senses the value of quiet as a welcome contrast to the usual compulsive chatter, the period may be extended to three or four minutes, or even longer. In any event, at the proper time the devotions leader begins to share with the group whatever material he or she has chosen: biblical readings, poetry, writings of a philosophic nature, an article from a contemporary magazine—in short, whatever may help to condition the group for the discussion which will follow. The leader then closes with brief prayer.

Now the discussion leader takes over. Initially he will review the substance of the assigned reading, summarizing the salient points before opening the meeting for questions, comments, and the sharing of insights. If participation by the group is slow in developing, he may pose some loaded questions. He may suggest that those present offer their views by going around the circle, each person in sequence having opportunity to speak. This device, incidentally, is of value where some in the group are eager to take over the conversation while others refrain from speaking up. If the assigned reading deals with several topics, the discussion leader may divide the group into two or more sections, each of which huddles in a different part of the room for a half-hour buzz session. At the end of that time they report their points of view as bases for further discussion by the entire group. Whatever technique is used, the discussion leader should be familiar with group dynamics. He should be sensitive to those persons who will express themselves only if encouraged, and he should be firm but tactful with those who try to monopolize.

At the proper time the leader closes off the discussion, usually by summarizing the highlights and defining areas which may require attention at another meeting. He then invites any of those present who may be facing problems during the next two weeks or who may know of others in difficult situations to voice these needs and concerns and to ask for the prayers of the group. Following this there is a period of meditation, during which anyone may offer a brief prayer. The leader usually concludes by leading the group in the Lord's Prayer.

There remain only the matters of deciding on the new assignment for study, the naming of the home at which the next meeting will be held, and the choosing of a devotion leader and a discussion leader, unless, of course, the group has designated a permanent discussion leader. The refreshment period which follows provides opportunity for additional unplanned discussions. In fact, in our *koinonia* group, the last person often leaves the host's home as late as midnight. But this is not recommended!

Please observe, Wayne, that a *koinonia* group is not simply a Bible-study group, or a discussion group, or a prayer group. True, it embodies all of these ingredients. But it must become much more. If the full dimensions of *koinonia* are to be experienced, it must grow into a closely knit fellowship in Christ, not unlike those early disciples who met in homes during the first century. It should be a group of people who weep with those who weep, rejoice with those who rejoice, and seek in every aspect of life to be agents of reconciliation, servants of their neighbor, and friends to the lonely and oppressed.

A big order, you say? You bet it is! And obviously, not all *koinonia* groups achieve this ideal. But perhaps we can best clarify their role in the twentieth-century American milieu if we try to define what *koinonia* groups are *not!*

First, *koinonia* groups *are not a substitute for the church.* Because worship takes place in the small group, it cannot be considered in lieu of corporate worship by the congregational family. Nor can attendance at *koinonia* meetings be an excuse for not taking part in the work of the church. *Koinonia* groups must be recognized as branches of the vine from which they derive their sustenance. Their mission is to enable people to experience intimate sharing through study and dialogue, so that they come to know other members of a Christian community in a way, and to an extent, which is impossible for the pew-sitter in a large congregation. Through *koinonia* groups, a person's church membership becomes more meaningful, more dedicated, and more deeply understood. When he has partaken of communion in the fellowship of the small group and in a home setting reminiscent of the upper room of Christ's day, the taking of communion in the larger fellowship of the church acquires a new significance. Moreover, the role of the church's liturgy as a means of affirming our belief and faith before man and before God may be difficult for some to grasp who have not participated in creating their own worship without a professional minister to lead them.

Second, *koinonia* groups *are not divisive influences which fracture a church congregation.* Quite the contrary. In our church, Wayne, as many as nine groups have operated simultaneously. They have spawned resource manpower for the entire church. From *koinonia* groups have come leaders who formerly declined to shoulder responsibilities, but who now gladly serve. Solidly grounded in the church's reason for existence, these individuals become the best reconcilers within the larger church family. They are the ones who support the ministers when the going gets rough. They are the ones who increase their financial support of the church, year after year. They are the ones who seek new avenues whereby the church may become more relevant to human need.

Third, *koinonia* groups *are not a form of psychological clinic.* They must not be used as a refuge, a means of evading the life for others which Christ demands of us all. Dietrich Bonhoeffer made this point clear:

Many people seek fellowship because they are afraid to be alone. Because they cannot stand loneliness, they are driven to seek the company of other people. There are Christians, too, who cannot endure being alone, who have had some bad experiences with themselves, who hope they will gain some help in association with others. They are generally disappointed. Then they blame the fellowship for what is really their own fault. The Christian community is not a spiritual sanatorium.*

But having acknowledged this, it should be pointed out that a *koinonia* group *can* heal many of the wounds which our hectic, impersonal life inflicts. In *koinonia* we come to know people in a way which can be found in very few, if any, of our other contacts. Here is where masks slowly drop and we reveal our true selves. We come to feel that we don't have to act, try to impress others, or put on a false front and in the process undermine our integrity. But note this, Wayne: Unless a person is willing ultimately to share with others on this frank and intensely personal basis, *koinonia* is not for him.

Sometime ago I was asked to speak about *koinonia* at a large suburban church. The occasion was the annual dinner meeting of the church's official family including its elders, deacons, trustees, and committee chairmen. As I sat at the speaker's table chatting with the senior minister, he pointed out the many prominent business executives in the audience—the president of a metropolitan bank, the senior vice-president of an insurance company, and a high official of a large electronics firm. Looking at these men, I began to wonder how many ever really could share with a small group their innermost uncertainties, hopes, and fears. They were intelligent, conscientious, highly motivated men; they were decision makers and influence wielders, the very men who so often are lonely simply because they are called upon to "have their guard up," that is, to fill the image expected of them.

When the time came for me to speak, I shared with them my experiences with *koinonia.* The audience was most cordial, seeming to strain to comprehend the significance of these unfamiliar ideas. At the conclusion of my talk they fired questions at me for a half hour or more. After the benediction, several of the younger men told me how much they craved the experience of participating in *koinonia,* if only a group could be formed in their church. Again and again I heard the plea: "I feel the need for this!"

Several months later I expressed to the minister my hope that the seeds had begun to bear fruit. He apologetically explained that the program of the church had been so hectic that they simply hadn't had time to start a *koinonia* group. But some day, he assured me, they would. In spite of his words he knew, and I knew, that they never will. For not only will the busywork of the church continue to take precedence over efforts to develop a more vital form of personal ministry, but the materially successful members of the congregation will be reluctant to venture into new and deeper waters.

Yet a hunger exists which is not being fed.

As Paul Tournier has said:

> It often happens that the doctor is the only one who in this modern world can offer an opportunity of personal fellowship. People expect him to understand them, for he has some experience of men and life, and because his training inclines him towards particular cases rather than general ideas, because he is an observer and not a theorist. It is to him that people are most willing to show themselves as they are. . . . I have met many doctors either attached to factories or practicing in working-class areas who were fully aware of the great mission entrusted to them. Into the privacy of their consulting-rooms come one after another men who never have an opportunity anywhere else of talking intimately.*

This is the sort of sympathetic atmosphere that a small group can effectively provide. When persons can have dialogue with concerned people who really listen, lives become changed and personalities which have become listless begin to blossom again. I have seen men and women whose marriages have been endangered by lack of meaningful communication begin to express within the *koinonia* family some of the frustrations they have been unable to voice in private to their marriage partners. The presence of the group has seemed to free these people to speak of their situation in a philosophic spirit, as though the problem were not unique to them (as, indeed, it isn't!). By using the group as a sounding board, one spouse begins to communicate obliquely with the other. Meanwhile, the group is drawn closer by the realization that often we can communicate least effectively with those we love most.

In other words, Wayne, a *koinonia* meeting ideally should have some of the aspects of a Halloween party, an "all saints" gathering without masks! For this is where the participants must seek to understand their real identities and to share that true self, without reservation, with the others of the fellowship. Indeed, the spirit of the gathering should be to "come as you are"—without pretense, without hypocrisy, trusting one another, sometimes resenting one another, but ultimately loving one another.

Sounds sort of refreshing, doesn't it?

Faithfully,

Ken

"If You Can't Live with Others, How Can You Live with Yourself?"

Dear Wayne:

Can *koinonia* become introverted and self-serving, you ask? Can it become a form of navel worship? Can it lead to exclusiveness, a sense of self-righteousness and pride? Can it become the antipathy of universal brotherhood?

I appreciate your sensitivity to dangers such as this, for these are precisely the questions a Christian should continually raise about his style of worship, his prayer life, and his church's priorities; namely, are they self-centered or are they God-centered?

Let me admit, at the outset, that *koinonia can* lead to smugness or clannishness. It *can* become an end in itself. But this must be avoided. As a group matures, it should be motivated toward forms of Christian service. In the words of George W. Webber:

> It must not be designed to make us more pious or simply to instill more knowledge about our faith. That has the effect of insulating us from the world or compartmentalizing our religious interest. The small group, as well as the corporate life of the church, exists not to stimulate or create koinonia but to prepare us for the mission of the church. But it is in the context of these two foci that, God willing, the fellowship of the church will become a reality.*

Now how does this work in actual practice? How do participants in *koinonia* groups avoid becoming excessively concerned with their own welfare? At what point do they go on mission?

I am glad to report that although some groups, like some individuals, take more than they are willing to give, such is not the usual pattern. Let me cite just a few examples of how *koinonia* can motivate people to a deeper sense of stewardship and commitment.

A director of research for a chemical firm became concerned about the deterioration of morale in his company. People no longer were sensitive to other people in their daily contacts. There was a calculated manipulation of others, an indifference to how things were accomplished, and a dehumanizing of people in the name of efficiency.

So he asked permission of his president to form a small group which would meet weekly in his office, at lunch time, for Bible study and discussion as to how Christ's teachings might be applied to their interpersonal relations. The president did not object. "If you can improve conditions," he said, "by all means go to it!"

In structuring this trial group, my friend adhered to an important fundamental: He invited men not from one, but from various departments of the company, and from various echelons: management, technical, clerical, and shop. Each participant brought a sandwich and my friend supplied coffee. So successful was this venture that before long a second group was meeting in his office on another day of the week. And later, still a third group was formed, not for Bible study but for discussion of enlightened personnel practices. Thus did a *koinonia* participant carry his lighted candle out into the "secular" world, lighting many other candles to remind men that God can be honored just as reverently and often more productively through a Christian approach to work situations than in the church building.

Another businessman saw an opportunity to witness to his faith when his company sent him to South Africa, prior to building a new manufacturing plant there. The purpose of his trip was to survey the labor market and existing rates of pay, so that a schedule of job categories and wage bands could be developed. Our *koinonia* friend was deeply disturbed by the wretched living conditions he found and the substandard rates of pay that were responsible for such squalor. On the plane back to the States he wrestled with this problem. If he recommended a rate structure no higher than the existing pattern, his firm could employ ample workers, obtain low labor costs, and show a fine profit. But this certainly would not be compatible with our friend's religious principles. So he drafted a report recommending a wage pattern substantially above the going rate, high enough to support a decent standard of living. In submitting it, he knew he was running a great risk. His management might logically say: "Here's a young man so idealistic he let his emotions outweigh his judgment. He'll never merit promotion to a higher echelon."

But, Wayne, our story had a happy ending. The firm's policy committee accepted his recommendations. As a result, a member of a *koinonia* group in Philadelphia, by his courage and faith, has blessed the lives of several hundred people in South Africa. True, he's not a missionary, in the conventional sense of the word. He's not talking about Christ or teaching about Christ, laudable as those occupations are. Instead, he's *doing* something for God's people and honoring Christ as a Christian layman "on mission."

There's an interesting sequel to this incident. As I write this letter, our friend is engaged in a survey, sponsored by a religious-lay group known as Metropolitan Associates of Philadelphia, involving the cooperation of the company for which he works. The aim is to determine how much of a reduction in corporate profits might be justified, from the ethical-economic point of view, on a product which could materially help underdeveloped countries to raise their standards of living. Isn't it an exciting evidence of business statesmanship that a corporation with sales in nine figures would lend itself to such a study, and that church people can thus influence decisions which have such a far-reaching effect on human life?

To supplement these examples of mission by individual *koinonia* members, let me mention briefly two examples of *koinonia* groups on mission.

One group from our church has worked with referrals from a state mental institution. These are patients who are discharged to return to "normal" living; they face a period of difficult adjustment without encouragement and friendship. The entire *koinonia* group was given instruction by staff psychiatrists at the hospital so that they might become sensitive to the psychological needs of the people they serve. As a result, members of the group were on call to provide support and companionship for recent dischargees. They went to shows with them, entertained them in their homes, made contacts with possible employers, and thus served as good neighbors. This form of mission performed inestimable good, and gave each member of the group a deeply satisfying feeling of involvement with fellow humans.

At Corning, New York, another *koinonia* group had been meeting regularly for four years without ever finding a viable form of mission. This troubled many in the group. Sensitive, dedicated persons, they found much strength in their association with one another. But always some deeper dimension seemed to be missing. Periodically they discussed their problem, without ever resolving it.

This situation led one of the couples in the group to contact us. Would Christine and I come to Corning and conduct a weekend retreat for the group? Might we perhaps serve as a catalyst so that the static ideas of the group could be shaken up, as in a kaleidoscope, and allowed to re-form in whatever pattern God might inspire? Would the coming of a new couple perhaps introduce some fresh element which might influence the dynamics of the group?

Such an invitation is always exciting and frightening. It is exciting because of the prospect of new friendships and the expectation of a spiritual encounter. It is frightening because of the realization of our inadequacies and the haunting fear that perhaps nothing creative may develop.

In planning for the weekend, we scheduled Bible study, presentations featuring various approaches to mission, probing questions to be pondered during intervals of silence, periods of discussion, and periods of prayer and meditation. All these were aimed at fostering an atmosphere of faith, expectancy, and openness to whatever creative impulses might flow into our consciousness. As the time to depart for Corning drew near, seldom have I prayed so earnestly for the Holy Spirit to use us in whatever way he saw fit to give new direction to the group's quest for mission.

And, Wayne, we had a thrilling experience. As happens only on special occasions, this retreat called into being a rare combination of eager, expectant people. We had a sensation of isolation such as you feel when a blizzard shuts you off from outside distractions and a warm sense of communion with others which can't begin to be described by so overworked a word as "fellowship." On this weekend, *everyone* felt drawn together into an intimate, sharing community. It was like a banquet, a feast, a celebration. When the retreat came to a climax with the serving of communion by the young minister in the group, we knew that our host, the Holy Spirit, was indeed present.

Now what do you think was the reaction of the participants after the glow had subsided? The woman who initiated the retreat reported in a letter:

> We've talked to different members about the retreat, and they all agree that our discussions had a depth and an openness that we'd never achieved before. The minister said, "This is the best thing my wife and I have done since we've been in Corning." Another man said, "We should do this about every six months." And as far as mission goes, we accomplished more than we have in four years, in a very practical sense.

But perhaps you're asking: "What ultimately happened as a result of the retreat? Was anything tangible *really* accomplished?"

For an answer, let's turn to some newspaper items in *The Corning Leader,* a year or so later.

Wednesday evening's open house program for "The Place," a downtown student center for Corning Community College students, was attended by between 100 and 150 students and adults, with attendance so good that the program was extended past the closing deadline.

Located on the top floor of the former English-Keenan building, now the Githler-Tanner building, on the corner of Pine St. and Denison Pkwy., the four-room center will be open from Monday through Thursday from 7 to 11 p.m. starting next week, it was decided Wednesday. . . .*

The project started with a couples' discussion group of the First Presbyterian Church over a year ago, when members, discussing various needs of the community, concluded that college students lacked an off-campus meeting place. Richard Kelly, a Corning Community College faculty member, was a member of the discussion group and relayed college viewpoints.

After much discussion with students, faculty and administration, the decision was made to go ahead with the plans. With William Hudson as general chairman and James Kullberg as treasurer, an organization was formed, consisting of an adult Board of Directors and a student board of governors. . . .

Following selection of the site, college students, faculty members and several interested adults worked with the original group in the cleaning, painting, floor-finishing and other necessary improvements.

Financing so far has been done by members of the group. Several interested individuals have reportedly promised future contributions and Treasurer Kullberg said it is hoped that others will give monetary support as time goes on.*

Observed *The Corning Leader* editorially:

With the lack of dormitories on the Spencer Hill Campus and the fact that many of the students live in the city area, this new venture offers something of the non-commercial variety to fill the vacuum which exists in the city for the college population. Once off the hill the students have little in the way of meeting places other than local bars and taverns. The Place offers a new location.

It's not elaborate, nor is it expansive. The Place was developed by a few local adults desiring to express the friendship and the concern of the community for CCC students. They are not the usual run-of-the-mill do-gooders, but rather people willing to assist and work with the students. The Place is the result. Students from the college made the major decisions in its development, contributed much in elbow-grease, energy, time and effort. They will make the major decisions in its operations.

It's refreshing to know that there is a place for youthful chit-chat, serious discussions among students and between students and faculty. The Place can be a center for relaxation and enjoyment and is long overdue.

So you see, Wayne, in scores of ways small groups are ministering to a diversity of people and needs. Far from being new, this is simply a modern counterpart of an almost forgotten Christian tradition in America. From colonial days to the industrial revolution, the nation's colleges, hospitals, homes for the aged, orphanages, and all manner of relief agencies were originated by small groups of concerned church people.

Before I end this letter, let me answer still another question you raised about *koinonia* groups. "How long do they function? Do they just fade away, like old soldiers, or are they terminated by mutual consent?"

There is no one answer to your query. Some groups meet for a few months, then disband because the participants feel they have grown in spiritual sensitivity and now prefer to spend their time in some form of service—tutoring one night a week, for example. Other groups may continue for years, then die out as people move away or drop out because of waning interest. Still other groups keep reconstituting themselves, new people coming in to replace those who leave, with the result that the orientation of the group and its specific objectives change with the passing years.

But remember, *koinonia* is not a fad, a passing fancy, or an oddball activity devised to bolster the flagging interest of church people. It is a basic requirement of a genuinely Christian church. Its origin is as old as the church itself. In fact, if we look upon Pentecost as the birth of the church, *koinonia* actually preceded it. For *koinonia* was the spirit of love and mutual concern which bound the disciples to Christ, as they met together in a small group to study, worship, and gain strength for *their* mission. If a church does not have *kerygma* and proclaim the gospel and challenge men to make it relevant; if it does not have *diakonia* and minister to those in need and become a reconciling force among men; and if it does not have *koinonia* and constitute a community which seeks to know and express God's love and forgiveness—then we must face the unpleasant fact that it is not in truth a church of Jesus Christ.

That's why, Wayne, we expose our new-member trainees to a *koinonia* experience during their period of indoctrination. Invariably many in the group express delight at finding something here they never before had encountered in a large church: an affectionate regard for them, quite apart from their race, their social or economic status, and their educational background. In a recent class for new members there was a young couple, personable and well educated, but obviously reticent and defensive in manner. They were warmly welcomed by the lay discussion leaders and accepted by all in the group. Soon their tenseness subsided, and they began to participate with enthusiasm. They felt surrounded by a spirit so genuine and supportive that they could relax, secure in the knowledge that they were among friends. Regrettably, this is not always the case when a wife is Caucasian and her husband Negro.

Now if the members of a *koinonia* group conscientiously live up to their commitments, and devote a period of each day to study, prayer, and meditation, their style of life can radically change their attitudes toward their secular life. But let's face it; not everyone is willing to do this. In fact, there are people who become terrified at the prospect of being alone for a half hour, with nothing to do or listen to but their own thoughts and the insights which God may inspire. It was of these people that Dietrich Bonhoeffer was thinking when he wrote:

> *Let him who cannot be alone beware of community.* He will only do harm to himself and to the community. Alone you stood before God when he called you; alone you had to answer that call; alone you had to struggle and pray; and alone you will die and give an account to God. . . .
>
> But the reverse is also true: *Let him who is not in community beware of being alone.* Into the community you were called, the call was not meant for you alone; in the community of the called you bear your cross, you struggle, you pray. You are not alone, even in death, and on the Last Day you will be only one member of the great congregation of Jesus Christ.*

You see, Wayne, this entire question of *koinonia* raises the fundamental question: "If you can't live with others, how can you live with yourself?"

The life of a Christian must inevitably be one of alternating rhythms. We are alone to shake things down with ourselves and with God, to re-think the situations we encounter when with others, to gain perspective, and to regain a sensitivity to human values. It is like recharging a battery. Then we are with others to listen and to comfort, to promote justice and reconciliation, to serve, and to be served. The body needs this change in rhythm, too, if it is to be renewed and revitalized. This is why we have sleep. The spirit needs it if our inner lives are to be renewed and revitalized. This is why we have prayer and meditation. For how else can we resist the contamination of temporal things? How else can we keep our consciences from being dulled, our ideals from being compromised, and our sensibilities from being hardened? The pressures to become something less than human are immense. The cult of conformity is hard to resist. The price tags placed on the world's goods, services, and loyalties can be debasing.

And if you think that we are not including church people among those for whom we are concerned, listen to the pungent and disturbing words of Thomas Kelly, a man who possessed rare spiritual insight:

> Some of the most active church leaders, well-known for their executive efficiency, people we have always admired, are shown, in the X-ray light of Eternity, to be agitated, half-committed, wistful, self-placating seekers, to whom the poise and serenity of the Everlasting have never come.*

Not very flattering, is it? But then, the truth seldom is!

I hope that if your minister starts a *koinonia* group, you will participate. Don't go into it with reservations. Don't be skeptical. Don't try to analyze every reaction and probe for the source of each motivation. Just open yourself to the Spirit.

As you have observed, I referred in this letter to retreats. They are a tremendous wellspring of inspiration to those willing to make an initial leap of faith. More about retreats in another letter, I hope.

In the meantime, Wayne, permit me to say, "God bless you." You may doubt that he cares, but I know that he does.

Faithfully,

Ken

"No Place for Sinners!"

Dear Wayne:

Sorry not to have responded to your last letter more promptly, but Christine and I have been out of town. In fact, we flew back East just last evening from Sioux Falls, after taking part in a most interesting ecumenical conference. There were about eighty-five ministers and laymen present from six denominations and a dozen states. It was a real privilege to be on a program with Bruce Larson, executive director of "Faith at Work"; Howard Keeley, director of the New England Evangelistic Association; and Roger Fredrikson, senior minister of the host church, the First Baptist Church of Sioux Falls. What inspiring, dedicated men these are! And what a spirited interchange took place on the final day of the session! By a strange coincidence, Wayne, it involved the rat-race aspects of the ministry which you and your pastor were discussing recently, according to your last letter. It was touched off by a question which revealed a deep-seated frustration.

"When I want to discuss something of importance with my husband," said a minister's wife, her voice dripping with despair, "I have to phone his secretary and ask for an appointment. I actually do! But what can I do about it?"

No one snickered. The plaint was symptomatic of pressures too universal, too disturbing. "I'm in the same bind," chimed in another wife. "My husband is on a seven-day-a-week merry-go-round of committee meetings, phone calls, counseling sessions, hospital visits, pastoral calls, sermon writing chores—you name it. And it never lets up. It's worse than being a golf widow."

"Yes, and that's not all," put in still another. "We aren't supposed to have a life of our own. When a parish buys our husband, it buys us too. Like a one-cent sale at a supermarket where the big jumbo double-package is offered for practically the price of one. We're expected to attend just about every social affair, sing in the choir, and give papers at the women's society meetings. It's a serious problem of identity. Are we persons—real people, or just a tail on a kite?"

All of which ties in with your observation, Wayne, that we laymen too often fail to see that our ministers and their wives *do* get a break. It's our responsibility, as you point out, to make certain that the pastor's schedule provides time off when he can be with his family and relax. On such days, lay people should cover for the pastor in all but emergency matters. Doubleheader meetings, such as a 7 or 7:30 P.M. meeting, followed by a 9 P.M. meeting, frequently can relieve both minister and laymen of another night out. To help free the minister's wife so that she, too, can enjoy this evening off, the women of the parish should meet with her for real dialogue about her need for identity and privacy and then take creative steps to protect it. A retreat for ministers' wives and women's society leaders from several churches might come to grips with this widespread occupational injustice.

Let me mention an innovation in one parish which is of significance to its co-ministers. A few years ago a member of this parish went to the ministers and said:

My family belonged to this church for many years but never, in my judgment, contributed as liberally as they could have done. So I'd like to initiate a special project. Ministers, like any other professional people, can easily go stale unless they have opportunity, from time to time, to acquire fresh perspectives. I'd like to finance an abbreviated sabbatical for one of our co-ministers and next year do the same for the other co-minister. If the church will grant them a two-month leave of absence, I'll pay for any approved program of study, research, or field observation up to a limit, say, of fifteen hundred dollars. But I want this to be anonymous.

What an imaginative layman! And what a fine opportunity for clergymen to keep on the cutting edge of the latest theological thought!

So you see, Wayne, it *is* possible, with imaginative lay leadership, to lift the minister's position to one of real professional stature and, at the same time, to give his wife her rightful status of "Wife, First Class" instead of "Parish Prisoner."

Incidentally, a somewhat amusing sidelight of the conference—and to me, a significant one—occurred when I was cornered in (of all places!) a men's washroom by two ministers from our audience. They proceeded to ply me with questions in a friendly but persistent way, in an effort to discover, as they put it, "what a layman really thinks about theological matters."

"What do you believe will happen to the person who does not accept Jesus Christ?" one of them asked.

Even I, a layman, recognized this as a loaded question. "If you are asking whether he will be consigned to eternal damnation," I replied, "it is my opinion he will not."

"But aren't we told that anyone who fails to accept Jesus Christ will perish?"

"Then what about a native of some far-off place who has never heard of Christ?" I asked. "Are you implying that he will be condemned? I understand that even the Roman Catholic church, which through the years has taken some very narrow positions on theological matters, has a belief that although a man may never have heard of Christ, if he has love in his heart and acts toward his fellowman in a Christlike manner, he is a spiritual follower of Christ, one who has been 'baptized in the spirit.' "

"But we're not referring to that type of situation," persisted one of my questioners. "We're concerned about the man who *has* been told of Christ, but refuses to accept him. Will *he* be deserving of eternal life? Will he have another chance?"

I drew a deep breath as I strove to marshal my thoughts. "Let me say first that I fear nobody actually can *deserve* eternal life." They watched me closely. "But in looking at this man's situation, isn't it important that we seek not to pass judgment upon him, but instead look at the total society of which he is a part? I would raise the question: 'Why has he rejected Christ?' Is it because the Christ presented to him is perhaps a caricature of the real Savior? Or has this man been so injured by injustice that he is bitter and incapable of hearing Christ's call? And if this is the case, where do *I* fit into this picture? May I not bear a considerable guilt in condoning a society where grave injustices prevail? By failing to reflect something of Christ's spirit in my relations with others, may I not have been instrumental in depriving him of Christ? And if this is true, is God's judgment really on this man, or is it on me and on others in our society?"

The ministers looked at me curiously. And then, with just a trace of irritation, one of them asked: "Then you don't believe that man has to make a choice? In other words, you feel that everybody will be saved; it makes little difference whether you live a good life or a bad life?"

"I guess I'll have to leave that up to God," I acknowledged. "But I do feel, first, that although man has a choice, it is not so free a choice that he can be held *solely* responsible for his decision. And second, that since we all are sinners, no one of us can escape some guilt for his brother's problems. And third, I hope that the true God—not the puny God we so often worship, but the all-creative Intelligence behind our universe— will be such a merciful Father that he will recognize that we are, in truth, really 'sons of God' and, however unworthy, we are privileged by the grace of Jesus Christ to receive forgiveness and be reconciled with our fellow- man and with God."

Ever since returning home from Sioux Falls, Wayne, I've been unable to dismiss this conversation from my mind. Like some haunting Bach theme, it keeps recurring amidst all the polyphonic running around of my secular life. On reflection, it seems to epitomize what has been one of the grave weaknesses of the Christian church down through the years— namely, its tendency to insist that it is infallible, that it has all the an- swers, and that it is composed of virtuous people who "have it made." The incident is reminiscent of the argument that arose between Peter and Paul, back in the earliest Christian community. Was the church only for Jews, or could it also embrace Gentiles? Scarcely had this been re- solved, freeing Paul to go to distant points to establish new churches for Jew and Gentile alike, before a similar conflict erupted among the new converts over who should be admitted. So widespread had been the custom of setting up all sorts of rules, regulations, and restrictions for membership in religious temples, they wanted to pass judgment on people and exclude those who did not meet *their* superficial criteria. In the four- teenth chapter of Romans, Paul admonishes these people, saying:

> As for the man who is weak in faith, welcome him, but not for disputes over opinions. One believes he may eat anything, while the weak man eats only vegetables. Let not him who eats despise him who abstains, and let not him who abstains pass judgment on him who eats; for God has welcomed him. Who are you to pass judgment on the servant of another? . . . None of us lives to himself, and none of us dies to himself. If we live, we live to the Lord, and if we die, we die to the Lord; so then, whether we live or whether we die, we are the Lord's. . . . Why do you pass judgment on your brother? Or you, why do you despise your brother? For we shall all stand before the judgment seat of God. . . . Then let us no more pass judgment on one another, but rather decide never to put a stumbling-block or hindrance in the way of a brother. . . . For the

kingdom of God does not mean food and drink but righteousness and peace and joy in the Holy Spirit; he who thus serves Christ is acceptable to God and approved by men (Romans 14:1-4, 7-8, 10, 13, 17-18).

I feel, Wayne, that some of your rebellion against the church and Christianity stems directly from the cult of exclusiveness that you often encounter among pious folk. Although no church, to my knowledge, actually has posted a sign above its doors "No place for sinners!" the message often is conveyed more subtly. Sometimes you can almost feel a spiritual early-warning system acting like a filter to screen out those sinners who happen to be poor, disadvantaged, black, or rejected by society. You sense that the person who asks the question, "Are you saved?" is really applying a superficial yardstick to the eternal dimensions of man's unworthiness and God's mysterious power to forgive. If you answer "yes" to such a question, you're in. But if you are sensitive to what is involved in accepting Christ and acknowledge with candor your daily failure *really* to follow him, by answering "I don't know," you're out!

During a lecture at Oxford University's Mansfield College, Christine and I heard Dr. George Caird cite an interesting anecdote which illumines this matter of salvation and grace. He said:

> There is a story told of a former Bishop of Durham that he was accosted one day by a member of the Salvation Army, who asked him: "Are you saved?" To which the bishop replied: "That depends on whether you mean in the past tense, the present tense, or the future tense. . . . If you mean "Did Christ die for me?", undoubtedly; if you mean "Are my feet firmly set upon the highway of salvation?", I trust so; but if you mean "Am I safe home in the blest kingdoms meek of joy and love?", certainly not. This story perfectly illustrates the threefold character of the New Testament doctrine of salvation. Salvation in the New Testament is always a past fact, a present experience, and a future hope.*

Another device used to keep a church congregation exclusive is to erect barriers based on doctrine. A church may insist that no person be admitted to membership unless he endorses every detail of, say, the Apostles' Creed. Or, by attaching great importance to the virgin birth, for example, such churches lose sight of the tremendous reality of God's gift to us in the person of Jesus, in the totality of his life, his death, and his resurrection. *These* are the facts about Christ which matter and not the details of his conception and birth, veiled as they are by such a lack of authentic data.

In the ultraconservative atmosphere of a Boston or a Philadelphia, modern counterparts of this senseless worship of sacred birth can still be found in the deference accorded ancestry as contrasted with accomplishment. Some years ago, in the apartment house where we then resided, lived a man who had never been gainfully employed throughout his entire lifetime. He didn't need to be. From his socially prominent forebears he had inherited considerable wealth. Freed of the necessity to work, this man might have devoted his talents to charitable activities. But he didn't. Instead he spent virtually every day in a nearby taproom which served him his breakfast, lunch, and dinner; the three meals were linked gastronomically by the imbibing of alcoholic beverages. His was not a lost weekend, but a succession of lost weeks. Yet when he was found dead in bed one morning, with liquor bottles strewn about his apartment, the metropolitan dailies featured his obituary on the front page. For it was not what he was or what he stood for that mattered in the eyes of the editors, but the mere fact of his illustrious antecedents, for which he was in no way responsible.

Still another way of feeling spiritually superior is to look upon minority groups as inferior and therefore not worthy of association with the church's elite. Recently a friend of mine found that the church he had joined ten years ago was becoming infected with this venom. Increasingly, people were speaking in disparaging terms of Negroes, Jews, and other ethnic groups. Obviously such persons would dilute the purity of this white, Anglo-Saxon, Protestant congregation.

In view of our Judeo-Christian heritage and his growing feeling of sympathy for the Jews as the anti-Semitism in the church became more blatant, my friend enrolled in a course given by a Jewish synagogue. There he found a friendliness and a refreshing absence of bigotry. Feeling frustrated, not with Christianity *per se* but with the lack of it in his church, he decided to become a Jew. While undergoing the transition he happened to visit our church and observed that we had Negroes, Orientals, an occasional Roman Catholic, and even an atheist or two in our congregation. One evening he sat in on our new-member class, listening intently to the new people as they spoke of what seemed true and valid in their religious experiences and what appeared to be pretentious and disturbing. He was entranced at this openness to one another, this willingness to admit doubts and to search for new avenues leading, hopefully, to deeper understanding. "I never knew there was a church like this!" he exclaimed enthusiastically. "Maybe I will have to rethink my future plans."

As I contemplate the church in action, I believe I see three principal symptoms which identify the cult of the exclusive:

First, *the institution is glorified at the expense of people.* Faced with a choice of spending money on a building or of alleviating some form of human misery, the decision invariably is to improve the structure.

This kind of thing was done by a Manhattan church not too many years ago, by squandering a small fortune simply to face-lift its facade. Similarly, ritual and liturgy are emphasized at the expense of ministering to people. A dramatically shocking example of this occurred some years ago at St. Patrick's Cathedral. The incident happened during a special mass celebrated with the assistance of certain prominent members of the laity. In the middle of the mass, one of these assisting laymen, a man of mature years, suddenly slumped to the floor of the chancel, not far from the altar. But no one moved to his aid. The mass continued without interruption. At its conclusion, attendants hastened to the prostrate form. Gently they rolled him over and sought to give help. But he was dead.

Second, *the church's ministry is focused on its own people, instead of on the world.* A proliferation of organizations and societies devote their energies to planning bazaars, entertainments, card parties, dances, dinners, and a host of similar activities. Although these are enjoyable and quite harmless, they are *not* ministries to people in need, the primary role of a servant church. Nor do they bring church members into direct nitty-gritty contact with our less fortunate brothers and their problems. As Martin Buber has observed: "So long as a man is set free only in his Self he can do the world neither weal nor woe; he does not concern the world. Only he who believes in the world is given power to enter into dealings with it, and if he gives himself to this he cannot remain godless." *

Third, *Christianity is regarded as a past-tense religion for a status-quo world, and not a dynamic way of life for an evolving world.* As a result, change is resisted bitterly. Experimentation is viewed with suspicion. Rites and liturgy continue to be used long after their original significance has vanished. Moreover, there is an unwillingness to develop new and creative forms which speak to modern man in modern idioms.

But although many churches still seem to worship the cult of the exclusive instead of the gospel of the universal, many walls and barriers, thank God, are being breached. Ecumenical collaboration is increasing at an exciting rate. Lay people are realizing that although pronouncements by the hierarchy endorsing ecumenism are important, only at the parish level can such pronouncements be sanctified by ventures in faith. The more we are separated from one another, the more we are separated from God. Consequently, I feel that *koinonia* groups are basic to the renewal of people and, through them, the church. For *koinonia* brings dissimilar peoples together in the context of a Christian community. It is not the end, but just the beginning. *Koinonia* is a means of providing new wineskins in which to pour the heady new wine of Christ's good news for *all* men.

This brings me again, Wayne, to your letter and the good news which *it* brought. How happy I am that your minister has started a *koinonia* group and that you and Margaret are in it! And how gracious it was of you to host the initial meeting! Wasn't it a new feeling to welcome people who were not coming simply to play bridge, see film slides, or chat about interesting but inconsequential things? I rather sense that you felt something you couldn't quite put into words, as though your home were being used for the first time for a purpose much greater than you could fully grasp; that in some mysterious way the common-place seemed to become uncommonly fresh and new, secular things and objects took on a touch of the sacred, and a strange sense of communion seemed to develop; almost as though, for the first time, what had always been locked up in a church sanctuary had now been permitted to break out and enter intimately into your home and into the everyday lives of all who were present. When you observed, "This is the first time I can ever remember anyone praying aloud in our home," you said more than words can convey.

I was delighted, too, at your rhetorical question, "Why hasn't someone started something like this before in our church?"

Many reasons might be cited: indifference, uncertainty as to how to get started, preoccupation with the busywork of the church, et cetera, et cetera. But for a less pleasant yet plausible reason, Wayne, listen to a letter I received recently from a seminary professor:

> Through my students I receive continual testimony of the effectiveness of the small intimate groups that here and there have made effective the work of the church. Of course, I have seen the forces of reaction discourage and suppress this type of Christianity, it seems, for the very reason that it is effective. There are many who do not want to expose themselves in order to live a more intense life and be rebuked by the lives of others who do this effectively.

The professor's observation may sound like an overstatement, but it isn't. A few years ago a ministerial friend of mine organized a *koinonia* group in his Southern parish. Within weeks hysterical voices were whispering: "Subversives!" "Radicals!" "They're the pastor's Communist cell!" The stigma stuck and the group disbanded.

Christianity never was easy, was it?

Faithfully,

Ken

"Before You Can Advance, Try Making a Retreat!"

Dear Wayne:

When I mentioned in a recent letter that Christine and I had led a retreat at Corning, New York, I anticipated that you might snort in derision in some future reply. You didn't disappoint me! Apparently the word "retreat" can send chills up and down the spines of many Protestant laymen, even those who look upon Roman Catholics as good friends. Perhaps to some, the word connotes black-robed friars with sad, ascetic faces, shuffling down dimly lighted corridors as they move silently from one form of self-denial to another. Your questions indicate that you are totally unfamiliar with what a retreat really is and what it seeks to accomplish.

"Why," you ask, "advocate retreats when throughout your letters you've been stressing the need to get out of the sanctuary and into the world? What purpose can be served by holing up like a groundhog in some remote spot? Why go in for a lot of pietistic nonsense? Sitting around glumly and thinking solemn thoughts! Starving yourself as if food and drink were something evil!"

When you pose questions like these, Wayne, I can see that your picture of a retreat comes straight from Hollywood. So permit me, out of my own personal experience, to share with you an unglamorized view of a typical Protestant retreat.

Just to clear the air, I should emphasize that retreats, like *koinonia* meetings, are not an end in themselves. If I have been talking on the one hand about ministering to our neighbor, and on the other about personal renewal of the spirit, these two are not incompatible. As Dietrich Bonhoeffer has affirmed, we must recognize our dual responsibility of living creatively with ourselves and also with others. So let's face it: Before we can advance, let's try making a retreat!

But, you ask, why? What is a retreat supposed to accomplish? And why do I say "make" a retreat?

Let's back up a bit and start at the beginning. First, there are many different types of retreats. At one extreme are those conducted in complete silence, usually in a monastery, to which our Roman Catholic brethren may come for a weekend of quiet, meditation, and reflection, based on reading and prayer. At the other extreme are work conferences which frequently are misleadingly billed as retreats. These meetings follow an agenda for the purpose of exploring, usually in depth, various courses of action which might be taken by a church, a denomination, or other religious body. I prefer to think of these latter sessions as conferences, not retreats.

Now the type of retreat I'd like you to become familiar with, Wayne, is neither the monastic type nor the conference type, but something in between. It makes use of quiet periods as well as discussion periods. It is led by one or more retreat leaders, but it depends in large measure for its effectiveness on the sharing of all who attend. This is why we say we "make" a retreat. Those who come make the retreat by their prayers, their presence, and their participation.

Basically this type of retreat is an experience in living together in community for a day-and-a-half or two days, often from a Friday evening to the following Sunday afternoon. The participants may comprise people from a church, a seminary, or a study group who already know each other. For these folk, the continuity of being together for as long as two days offers opportunity for deeper levels of sharing than shorter meetings can provide. On the other hand, the participants may be strangers, drawn to the retreat by the invitation of friends, by a special interest in the theme announced for the retreat, or by the reputation of the leader or leaders.

Such a retreat can be for men only, for women only, or for married couples and single persons of both sexes. Its theme can be general, like "How can we deepen our prayer life?" or "How can a Christian witness in his daily work?" Or the theme can be so specialized that it appeals to specific categories of participants. The question, "How can minister and layman work together with more understanding?" can bring together clergy and laity for the type of heart-to-heart dialogue which rarely can take place during the hustle-bustle of daily parish life. "What are the criteria for a Christian marriage?" can give married folk and engaged couples an opportunity of exploring aspects of married life which are only touched on lightly in magazine articles and seldom are the basis for genuine dialogue. "The medical profession and Christian ethics" can help physicians to dissect the many aspects of their profession which involve ethical decisions and the welfare of their patients. Other retreat topics may appeal especially to businessmen, lawyers, seminarians, or teachers.

As you will appreciate, Wayne, the retreat leader's background must qualify him to be a resource person for the topic to be discussed. He must prepare painstakingly so that he can guide the thinking of the group along orderly, logical lines. He must understand group dynamics and be sensitive to the psychological needs of various types of people. He must have faith in God, a respect and love for people, and the humility to realize that if those present are to experience renewal, it can only come about through the working of the Holy Spirit.

The other essential ingredients are a retreat center sufficiently isolated to be free of distractions, a supply of inspirational books for those who wish to read during quiet periods, a bit of unspoiled nature for any who would like a short hike through woods or across country, an adequate provision for plain but tasty meals, and a group of retreatants—fifteen to twenty in number—who come with open minds and an expectation that God might touch their lives in some new and exciting ways.

Suppose I acquaint you with the conduct of a retreat by describing what takes place during a typical day-and-a-half experience of life together. Let's assume that we are attending a retreat at Kirkridge, an interdenominational center in the Pocono Mountains of Pennsylvania. To Kirkridge come people from all parts of the United States and Canada. There are groups from parish churches, denominational boards and divisions, colleges and seminaries, and individuals engaged in a variety of political, labor, business, and professional activities. An old farmhouse on the three-hundred-acre Kirkridge property has been progressively enlarged, without destroying its mellow charm, until it now provides sleeping accommodations for more than a score of people. Up on the mountain top, a half mile or so from the main building, is a modern lodge with dining and sleeping facilities for about ten people and with an expansive view of the surrounding country.

We arrive from the city about six o'clock on a Friday evening, park the car, and carry our sparse luggage up the flagstone walk to the entrance. People are encouraged to bring a minimum of clothes and encumbrances with them and *no briefcases!* Stepping inside, we find that others already have arrived. Standing or sitting in small groups are a dozen men and women, some getting acquainted, others renewing friendships and conversing animatedly. The leader of the retreat greets us and suggests we explore the dormitory area, taking whatever accommodations appeal to us. Rooms are allocated on a first-come, first-served basis.

The bedrooms are small and severely plain, but clean and neat. Some have two single beds; a few have only one. We stow away our belongings (sweater, slacks, and loafers are the order of the day) and return to the main room.

A fire is crackling in the big, stone fireplace, casting a cheery glow over the exposed beams of the ceiling and the shiny random-width floor. We glimpse rows of bookshelves, sagging with the weight of scores of inviting volumes. Above the fireplace mantel is the Kirkridge cross, an inconspicuous but significant symbol which suggests a presence as warm as the flames below. On the walls hang interesting prints and tapestries, examples of the arts and craft work of talented people who have spent time here. There is a refreshing absence of radios, television sets, and other distracting elements of modern living. In fact, you can feel the quiet simplicity, the lack of pretense, the honest authenticity of this place, so rich with the memories of past generations who have come here seeking insight into the eternal mysteries of life and death and rebirth.

The retreat leader introduces us to the others. They represent a diversity of ages and backgrounds, but they display friendliness and warmth. Their manner suggests a desire to relate to people on some deeper, more personal level than is possible in most purely social contacts. In fact, you are struck by the absence of small talk. These people truly seem to be seeking to understand who this person facing them really is.

Someone suggests that we examine the work assignment schedule on the bulletin board. It provides spaces for volunteers to sign up to help prepare breakfast, to set tables and serve one or more meals, and to clear off the tables and do K. P. duty. We dutifully sign up and walk away with a slightly magnanimous feeling.

The atmosphere is casual and relaxing as we come together for our plain but appetizing evening meal, prepared by Kirkridge's talented cook. Sitting at two large rough-hewn tables, in this rustic room, we feel our customary pace slowing down to a pleasant, almost medieval tempo.

Some time after dinner, we gather in a large circle for the initial get-acquainted session. The lights are dim and a soft glow from the fireplace fills the room. Our leader reviews the procedure to be followed during the retreat, the books which we will use as resource material (some of which we had been urged to read before coming), and something about what we hope may be accomplished during this weekend together.

Each person in the circle now is invited to introduce himself, to tell something of his vocation, his interests, and the reasons which impelled him to come on the retreat, as well as anything he cares to share regarding his spiritual pilgrimage. As person after person speaks, some eloquently, some haltingly, many as though they were articulating inner thoughts for the first time, we begin to sense that each person's quest is, to some degree, a reflection of our own. As the evening moves on, we seem to be drawn closer together.

Before we know it, ten o'clock is approaching and the leader conducts brief devotions. All of us participate in a short responsive reading and in the singing of the evening hymn. We will now observe silence until the next morning *after* breakfast. For many this is a new experience. How strange it is to retire silently, with only smiles and friendly nods to one another as we file out, some taking along books for a last bit of reading before turning in!

We arise the next morning to the sizzle of frying bacon and the tangy aroma of freshly-made coffee. One by one the retreatants put in their appearances, some emerging from the corridor of the dormitory wing, others coming in from the outside where they have been enjoying the clear, crisp, early-morning air. As the breakfast bell summons the stragglers, we gather around the two tables, waiting for the saying of grace by one of the group. Then, for many, comes the new experience of communicating with others during breakfast by signs, gestures, nudges, and smiles. What a brotherly spirit of comradeship develops as we begin to learn that in silence there can be deeper levels of communication than through speech! As we sit there eating, we begin to realize that all the chatter we would normally be indulging in really would add little, if anything, to the day. How much of our conversation is compulsive, simply because we feel uneasy at *not* expressing unasked-for opinions! And how often this chatter shuts out creative thought and worthwhile ideas!

After breakfast, the group reconvenes for the first session. The silence is broken by the leader who presents the topic for initial discussion, and a peculiar feeling comes over us. When we are ready to speak, we find ourselves screening our ideas much more carefully than before. Now words are seen to have value, if wisely chosen, and are not to be squandered profligately, but to be laid before others thoughtfully and responsibly, with respect for the listener's prerogatives and sensibilities.

After the leader's initial exposition, discussion gets under way, and the group gradually comes to grips with some of the deeper aspects of the subject. As people become a more integral part of the family, reserves melt away and remarkably frank incidents are related to illustrate attitudes, opinions, or pertinent problems. In this climate of trust, no one feels called upon to justify, defend, or apologize for a point of view.

The midday meal is eaten in silence, except for the voice of a reader sitting at the end of one table, who shares from an inspirational book while all listen quietly and reflectively. The early afternoon has free time to be spent in reading, meditation, hiking, or going off with a group to cut wood for the fireplace. The physical activity of working in silence with a congenial group is also a form of sharing which further binds us together.

The late afternoon session is not unlike the morning meeting, except that as the feeling of community strengthens, the discussion becomes more intense. At dinner, conversation is in order. With restrictions lifted, the interchange of ideas fairly sparkles. The evening discussion period follows somewhat the pattern of the others. The worship period then leads to silence for the remainder of the evening and until after breakfast on Sunday.

The unique and climactic experience of the retreat on Sunday morning is the worship service, which is created entirely by the retreatants. On the night before, the retreat leader has made assignments to various of the participants. After the opening words by the leader and the singing of a hymn, one of the group leads the service in adoration, using scriptural readings of his choice and a brief meditation. Another continues with the confessional portion of the service, followed by others expressing thanksgiving, intercession, and consecration. Then comes the climax of the service as the celebration of communion takes place by the passing of bread around the circle from person to person, followed by the passing of the communion chalice. During this celebration, everybody present offers silent prayer for each member of the group as that person partakes of the elements.

When the moment arrives for the group to leave Kirkridge, there is the realization that in less than two days these people who were strangers, or, at best, casual acquaintances, have mysteriously coalesced into a closely knit community, so united by the bonds of the Spirit that it is only with the greatest reluctance that the various individuals tear themselves away. This reaction to an initial retreat experience is not unusual. Observes a Lutheran layman of his first retreat:

Change, growth, love, sharing, peace, and a greater closeness to God; all these things and many more were discovered during this glorious experience. A spiritual communion with each other (never before experienced) which flowered during periods of silence became very real and meaningful. Among our group, the members of which were complete strangers before assembling for this retreat, there very quickly developed a surprising feeling of closeness, a feeling of love, a feeling of understanding and from this, I feel, each and every one of us came to have a new look, a new life, and perhaps even a feeling of rebirth.

Agrees a woman who, with her husband, had just attended her first retreat:

This was, as we probably said, our first retreat, and we were certainly glad we braved the "nonconformist" situation to come to Kirkridge. Both of us felt enriched by that brief experience, in ways that are difficult to explain to those of our friends who ask about it.

Yes, a retreat experience and a *koinonia* experience *are* difficult to explain to others. And yet, isn't this simply what the parish church, in essence, should be? As a Presbyterian woman said, after looking at a photograph of the people with whom she had shared her first retreat:

The bonds of community remain, and we look at the photo with a warmth of feeling that continues to surprise us. What power the church would have if this feeling of love, sharing, interdependence, and presence of the Holy Spirit among us were to become the climate of the average congregation!

Such experiences raise the question: How is this to be accomplished? Are retreats of any value in helping to bring about such a renaissance? Can lay people be effective in cultivating this sense of belonging to a family in Christ? Can they really become the leaven in the parish-church loaf, the salt which has not lost its savor?

One layman who was deeply stirred by his first retreat believes that this *can* happen. He writes:

This weekend has been one of real enlightenment to me. I think we experienced here some of the fellowship of the very young Christian community—a real sense of oneness in Christ. It was also refreshing to see real concern for and dedication to the Christian life by laymen. With people like this sprinkled throughout the church and hungry for this unity of spirit, the whole organized church has great opportunity to be reawakened to its real purpose and revitalized, so it can again become the living Body of Christ as Paul envisioned.

This point of view was supported by another participant, who feels that laymen *can* do an important part of the job and thus relieve ministers of this heavy burden. Speaking of his initial exposure to a retreat, he said:

> This experience has convinced me that dialogue can bring meaningful interpretations of God's Word to those interested, and that it can be done by laymen with less theological background than I had supposed necessary. Guidance from a pastor and the Holy Spirit for a group of leaders can thus spread Bible study much faster than is done by our conventional methods.

And that, Wayne, is one of the prime reasons why retreats are so valuable. They begin to equip people to serve others. They can become, in effect, a training ground for lay ministers. Sensitive lay people who are exposed to this sort of encounter begin to feel the authenticity of Jesus Christ and the power possessed by those who can witness to his lordship. As a layman just coming from his first retreat put it: "We cannot continue to try to lead others to God until we ourselves are filled with the Holy Spirit and feel secure enough in our faith to share it. Maybe this is why our educational program is not what we think it should be." A penetrating observation, that! "People long for fulfillment," he continued. "What help do they really get? Seeing the depth of faith that these people had here is something I have never seen in our church. I'm sure people have it—they just cannot share it."

Actually, retreats work different miracles with different people. I have already commented, Wayne, about the effect of silence on people. Relieved of the compulsion to talk, talk, talk, individuals often find that they listen to others with new perception. One layman confessed with admirable candor:

> Never have I said less and learned more about my associates than I did this weekend. Through my inward sensation (unknown to me) I have felt their desires and sensed their needs which ultimately were revealed to be my spiritual desires and needs. This is amazing. Upon arriving at Camp Luther I was dubious of what I was in for, but I was determined to enter into this retreat wholeheartedly. I am glad I did. If personal gain is to be recorded as a percent of profit, it would be an astronomical figure approaching infinity.

Note, if you will, that this man was dubious of what he was "in for" when he ventured to his first retreat. His reaction was typical. We all shy away from the unknown. To many, a "retreat" seems such an oddball sort of activity that they fear ridicule from their friends. But as I've said before, a leap of faith is essential to almost any forward movement.

Some laymen approach their first retreat, not with misgivings, but with a spirit of optimism and excitement. Such a man wrote:

I came not knowing what to expect. An adventure, I thought. This retreat turned out to be an adventure in Christian living, learning, and fellowship. Learning from my own experiences with God, as well as hearing other people's thoughts. Shyness and backwardness soon disappeared. We soon were able to express sincere thoughts and ask for help and understanding.

Note an important phrase this man used: "Hearing other people's thoughts." Often we church people don't listen. Our church organization is structured along such formal, impersonal lines that we have little opportunity to enter into genuine depth relationships. Nevertheless, people have a hunger for just this sort of sharing. Hear the words of gratitude from a woman who felt the power of personal witness:

You were truly an evangelist when you came to our retreat and gave of yourself in the telling of your personal spiritual growth. I cannot describe the great impact this made and how stirring it was to hear you tell it. Surely this retreat brought about a change in all of us.

Retreats can bring about a change, too, in the relationship between minister and lay people. The professional minister can be a very lonely man. He longs to be able to confide in lay people, assured of their discretion and their affection. The layman needs to be able to work with his minister as a trusted friend, seeking the direction needed to make his life more effective and fulfilling. Listen to how this type of relationship began to grow between a young minister and two of his laymen who had attended a clergy-laity retreat, and were driving home together. The minister wrote:

The return trip with Larry and Jim was an extension of the *koinonia* we shared at Kirkridge. Our trip was safe and uneventful from the standpoint of our physical well-being. Spiritually, it was exhilarating, a time of deepening and broadening our knowledge of one another. So together were we in the Spirit that Jim said to me, "Jerry, why are you so tense about your job?" We decided that my anxiety to do a good job was one of the reasons I might not be making as much progress as I would like in my relationship with some of the senior high youth. Until Sunday afternoon I hadn't considered that possibility. When we delivered Larry, holding him by the arm, with Jim toting a piece of flagstone we picked up at Kirkridge and dubbed "Larry's headstone," Adeline hesitantly opened the door to let us in. She said, "If I didn't know better, I would think you all had been drinking." I can understand how Peter and the disciples must have been considered drunk at Pentecost. A bond of fellowship has been fashioned among the three of us that will enable us to leaven the life of the church in some significant ways, I am sure.

Another minister, who found this clergy-laity retreat significant to him and to the layman who accompanied him, writes:

I was particularly interested in the reaction that Dick had to the retreat. I thought he made some rather helpful contributions, and it was clear to me that he came home benefiting in a number of important ways. This, I believe, is the real advantage of such a clergy-lay retreat, and I know that great things will be in store for us as we continue to work together in the future program of the church.

And finally, Wayne, one last comment. To me, the sacraments of the church too often seem overinstitutionalized by elaborate settings, and depersonalized by the physical presence of so many participants. As a result, the intimate meaning of communion, the sense in which it is celebrating a supper or a feast, eludes most people. That's why I consider it imperative that communion be offered from time to time within the context of *koinonia* groups and retreats. Hear the reaction of one layman to his first experience of sharing communion in a small group:

> The communion service was particularly meaningful in a retreat setting. Never had I experienced the sacrament in greater simplicity; never have I experienced communion in the fullest sense of the term. When my turn to partake arrived, I felt a sense of inner quietness and strength I cannot recall having sensed before.

Since you are such a discerning fellow, Wayne, by this time you've realized that I have been firing all the heavy artillery I could marshal in the hope that your resistance to anything as "silly" as a retreat might crumble. I do feel that before you can advance further, maybe you *should* participate in a retreat!

But what, you may ask, does a retreat ultimately accomplish?

The key to your question, I suspect, is the word "ultimately." My answer, honestly and simply, is, "I don't know." God works in mysterious, and often devious, ways. Frequently seeds may seem to fall on barren ground. Yet, at some later time, those seeds have a way of blossoming forth in an amazing way. And the time gap between the planting of the seed and its flowering may make the two seem unrelated. But I have faith that ultimately—*ultimately*, Wayne—all things work for good.

I could tell you about the two young women from our church and the way a retreat radically changed their plans, their lives, and the lives of many, many other people. But that is too long a story for this letter.

By the way, is it true that you and Margaret are planning a trip abroad? It sounds exciting. Here's hoping you make it, Wayne?

Faithfully,

Ken

"You Can't Go on Mission Without Traveling!"

Dear Wayne:

So you really got off to Europe! You finally decided to "see how the other half lives," as you put it. Your postcards have been arriving every few days, pinpointing your progress. How happy I am that you and Margaret are having the enriching experience of seeing other lands, mingling with other types of people, getting the feel of other modes of life! When one stays in his own little enclave, associating chiefly with persons who have similar ideas and aspirations, he tends to create a private world which becomes more and more distorted as he manipulates it to accommodate his fears, prejudices, and inadequacies. Less and less is he in touch with the true realities of God's universe.

In this sense, travel has a religious dimension. It is especially so if we journey to countries which have different languages and customs. In a thousand ways, we begin to sense that we are indeed strangers and so-journers on this earth. Because we cannot summon old friends whenever we want to, we begin to seek new ways of making friends of others. We realize, perhaps for the first time, the spiritual truth that each of us does, indeed, need others.

Being unfamiliar with the idioms of a foreign language, we observe other people with a new intensity, searching their faces for clues to meaning. We begin to *see* the person with whom we are thrown into contact, and in the process we become more sensitive to the common humanity in *all* people. Because we are separated from the resources of our provincial little world back home, we find ourselves rearranging our values, assigning great importance to hitherto overlooked aspects of life, and at the same time, sloughing off many sacred cows which once appeared essential to the Good Life.

And that is why, Wayne, anyone really serious about serving people less fortunate must realize, sooner or later, that you can't go on mission without traveling!

In fact, travel becomes the first essential step in mission, whether one journeys five miles into an underprivileged area of an American city or five thousand miles to a strange land. In this sense, travel means moving out from the familiar, leaving the habit-deepened ruts of daily life. Travel also calls for psychological reorientation, being receptive to new thought patterns and attitudes. And it calls for spiritual resensitizing; the faith to risk new encounters; an acceptance of the think-ye-not-of-the-morrow philosophy.

I can almost hear you demand, Wayne, "Please, *please* be more specific! How can you compare traveling in a foreign country with going on mission in an American city? If I go to France, I have a language problem and I know it. But if I go to an underprivileged neighborhood in New York, Chicago, or Los Angeles, at least I don't have that problem to worry about. We all talk the same language, don't we?"

The answer, of course, is a resounding "No!" How can a white, middle-class, Anglo-Saxon Protestant do-gooder really speak the same language of, say, a black, underprivileged, unchurched Afro-American? Let me cite just a few examples of what I mean.

Explains a do-gooder to a group of residents of a ghetto: "Friends, I have just been down to the Board of Health to tell them about the terrible rat situation on your block and I got a sympathetic ear. In fact, they've promised to send a sanitation truck and a crew of exterminators out here next week. They'll seal off the rat nests, inject cyanide gas, and clean out the place. Isn't that good news?"

With a pleased smile, he waits to receive the thanks of these new friends. But instead there is a frenzied babble of voices. "Don't you do that, man! Don't let those no-good sanitation guys come down here. We don't want them. Keep them out!"

The do-gooder blinks in amazement. "You mean you don't want to get rid of the rats?"

"Sure, we want to get rid of the rats!" shouts back a chorus of voices. "But you know what? One of those no-good housing inspectors, he'll come too. And he'll snoop, and he'll see we've got eighteen people living in one house. And he'll say, 'You're breaking the law. You've got three families in this house. No good. Two families have to go.'" There is an expressive pause. "Go where? We ain't got no place to go! We don't have money to get houses for each family." Then a stern admonition, supported by threatening gestures: "Look, man! You call them guys off. Understand? We don't like rats, but if rats go, we go. So we stay, and the rats stay too."

You see, Wayne, an *economic chasm* can separate people and make dialogue difficult.

Or consider the teacher newly assigned to a school in an underprivileged area. Little Arnold, she finds, can never quite grasp the meaning of many of the words she uses. So one day she visits the boy's mother to discuss the problem. "Can't you get Arnold to look up some of those words in your encyclopedia?" suggests the teacher brightly. "If he could see pictures with the words, he would learn more quickly."

"In a—a—what?" asks the mother haltingly.

"An encyclopedia, a book with information about all sorts of things."

The mother sighs. "Sorry, miss. We don't have books. We *never* have books. Maybe Arnold, he needs a book. You think so?"

Yes, Wayne, an *educational chasm* can separate people and make dialogue difficult.

Or consider the conversation in a church school class where the teacher is trying to stress the importance of prayer and thankfulness. "Jennie," she asks of a little pig-tailed youngster, "when you and your brothers sit down to dinner at night, you say grace, don't you?"

Jennie's big eyes fairly pop. "Say grace? We don't say no grace."

"You don't? But why not?"

"We don't sit down for dinner, like you say." Jennie gestures animatedly. "We have a pot on the stove. Maybe spaghetti, maybe cereal, sometimes." She grins in happy remembrance. "Sometimes maybe stew. That's good. So when we're hungry, we go to the stove and get food and eat at the kitchen table, maybe. Or on the floor in front of TV. But we don't all sit around no table, Miss Betty. We don't have no grace."

In other words, Wayne, a *cultural chasm* often separates people, making dialogue difficult.

Or finally, consider the young minister who is trying to explain to a very small boy something about the nature of God. "Stanley, God really loves you," he tells him with a friendly smile. "He really does. God is your heavenly Father. Do you understand?

The little boy's eyes narrow and his lips tighten. "You say God loves me, man? Come off it! You say he's my father? Then I hate God!"

"Hate God!" The minister's brow furrows and he shakes his head. "Don't say that, Stanley. You really don't hate God."

"Yes, I do," persists the small boy vehemently. "My father, he gets high. He beats my old lady. A no-good bastard, he is. I hate my father. I hate God!"

As you can see, Wayne, a *religious chasm* can separate people and make dialogue difficult.

Actually, then, the five miles separating a suburban area from an urban ghetto may represent a greater distance to cover, intellectually, emotionally, and spiritually, than the five-thousand mile gap between America and a point in Africa. In addition, there is the built-in feeling of superiority which too often we feel when in contact with so-called underprivileged people. Yet some of these folks have more to teach us than we have to teach them. Facing misfortunes which would send many suburbanites scurrying to their psychiatrists, these people show courage, fortitude, and stamina which command admiration and even envy. In fact, I will venture an opinion (which many might bitterly resent) that God often is present in a deeper, more real sense amidst all the poverty and misery of the slums than he is in some affluent communities of suburbia. I feel certain that if Christ were physically among us today, the slums are the places we would most often find him!

Now does all this talk about economic, educational, cultural, and religious chasms suggest that we cannot befriend underprivileged people? Definitely not! But it *does* indicate that instead of approaching them with a condescending spirit, the do-gooder would be well advised to approach with humbleness, compassion, and a willingness to listen, listen, listen, not only with his ears, but also with his heart. Let me cite an example of what I mean.

A few years ago in my own church a number of us sought to become more relevant to the needs of our changing community. Many felt that we should start a day nursery for working mothers. Why not equip a room in our commodious education building, engage qualified people to serve as teachers, and embark on a program?

Fortunately, someone suggested that we first hold a meeting of block leaders from the surrounding neighborhood. These were men and women designated by the local residents to take leadership in any matters affecting their blocks. Such a meeting was arranged. About ten or twelve of these block leaders, most of them Negroes, came to our church on an appointed evening. Also present were our co-ministers and people from appropriate committees of the church.

For almost a half hour there was polite but guarded conversation as various of our church leaders outlined how the project might be set up. Then one of the Negro block leaders got to his feet and brought all conversation to a halt by the intensity of his manner and the piercing quality of his gaze.

"Before we go any further," he said, with challenging directness, "I want to know one thing. Do you folks really plan to take action, or do you just want to talk? I attend a lot of meetings with white people. I hear a lot of pretty speeches. But usually they don't end up meaning nothing. I don't want to hurt nobody's feelings, but if that's the way it's going to be, I think we ought to know it now."

He sat down. For a moment there was silence. Then the tension suddenly lifted and there was a sigh almost of relief. Said one of our church leaders: "You raise a good question, and we respect you for it. We invited you here because we really do want to get action. We want to help our community. But frankly, we aren't sure just what we should be doing. I can see that we've been talking too much. Instead, we should be listening. We'll appreciate it if you'll take over and give us *your* ideas and advice."

With that, the climate changed. Monologue was replaced with genuine dialogue. The block leaders were doubtful as to how many working mothers in the neighborhood really would avail themselves of a day nursery. But since they didn't know, they volunteered to canvass their respective blocks and report back.

The upshot was that only three or four mothers in a ten or twelve block area expressed any real need for a day nursery. Instead, they were seriously concerned about the high drop-out rate among students attending the high school, directly across the street from our church. "Without education," many of the mothers said, "our kids just aren't going to get ahead. But they're having difficulty keeping up with their class. If only they could be helped, it would put an end to one of our great worries."

And so we formed, not a nursery school staff, but a tutoring staff. Before long, as many as twenty adults from our membership were coming to the church every Monday evening to tutor, usually on a one-to-one basis, some sixty teen-agers who desperately needed guidance in their studies. And at the end of the year, it was gratifying to find that a large percentage of these young people had made the grade academically.

This incident, Wayne, illustrates the crucial importance of having dialogue with the world and really listening. How can the church do God's work if its members fail to hear God speaking to them through the voice of the person in need? And to hear requires not only attentive ears, but also a heart sensitive enough to detect the unspoken plea behind the words. For often in the need which is *not* expressed we find the key to understanding a brother.

But if the church often fails to have dialogue with the less privileged members of society, it can be equally negligent of the most creative people in our culture, such as the artist, the poet, the dramatist, and the musician. I thought of this when we began to receive postcards from you and Margaret picturing famous cathedrals. Fancy you, a one-time atheist, sending us views of Cologne, Notre Dame, Chartres, and Saint Peter's! Of these, the handsome picture of the Chartres Cathedral was most nostalgic. Looking at it, I remembered threading our way along the narrow streets of the old village, suddenly coming upon the base of the towering cathedral, with all those little craft shops and studios clustered around it, signifying the close alliance which the artist, the artisan, and the craftsman once had with the church. In fact, this was in a special sense *their* cathedral, because they helped to design and erect it as an expression of their adoration of God. And inside were the statues, the friezes, the carvings, the stained glass, the tapestries, the frescoes, and the paintings, representing the finest creative talent of that day.

By contrast, today's most creative individuals are often *outside* the church. Yet the artist is a sensitive person through whom God may make known, in peculiarly moving and penetrating ways, some of his most cogent truths. As a result, the church is infinitely poorer and less creative due to this lack of communication, while the arts may be oblivious to certain dimensions of eternity which dialogue with the church might provide.

But this chasm between churchman and artist *can* be bridged. It *is* possible for both to find a common meeting place where each can enrich the life of the other. At our church, for example, one of our co-ministers, Theodore W. Loder, formed a "Listening to the World" discussion group. Its members read the works of contemporary and classical dramatists, novelists, and poets; then they meet together to search out the truths about themselves and about God as revealed by these artists. Soon it became necessary to organize a second group, because our people were so interested in reading and dissecting writers like Camus, Ibsen, Albee, and Baldwin.

To bring together the layman and the artist in more direct confrontation, our church has staged several religious arts festivals, planned and presented by our Fine Arts Committee and our Director of Fine Arts, Louise Curry Wakefield. The most recent festival, a week-long extravaganza, began with an interpretative dance in the sanctuary during the regular Sunday morning worship service. In the afternoon a special jazz worship service was presented by Pastor John Gensel, Lutheran minister to the jazz community of New York City, and an ensemble directed by trumpeter Joe Newman, composer and recording artist. This service combined Scripture and musical improvisation in a reverent manner which was a revelation to many who attended. Following the service, a reception was held for the professional artists, students, amateurs, and child artists whose oil paintings, watercolors, prints, etchings, wood carvings, and sculpture were on exhibit in the church's galleries throughout the week.

During the evenings of this busy period, the church's buildings were thronged by all sorts of people who came to hear—and talk with—our guest artists: Poet John Ciardi of *The Saturday Review;* Eleanor and Frank Perry, producers of the prize-winning film *David and Lisa,* who showed another of their films, *Lady Bug, Lady Bug,* and monitored a discussion based on its message; Rev. Al Carmines of the Judson Memorial Church in Greenwich Village and members of the Judson Players who staged interpretative skits; and workshop sessions on drama, led by Norman Newburg, and on dance, featuring Audrey Bookspan.

On two consecutive evenings in the sanctuary James Forsyth's drama *Heloise* was presented by a cast composed of members of the church and some professionals. The climax of the festival was a rendition of Carl Orff's "Carmina Burana" by an eighty-five-voice chorus, a forty-five-piece orchestra, and professional soloists.

Wayne, I wish you could have visited the coffee shop in the basement of the church and shared in the informal entertainment, refreshments, and fellowship after several of the performances. You would have found the place thronged with an unusual variety of folk—artists with and without beards, teen-agers in all sorts of garb, conservatively dressed oldsters, church members, and people who hadn't been inside a church for years, Protestants, Catholics, and Jews, whites, Negroes, and Orientals. There was a universality about the crowd which you would have found stimulating. Here were people of dramatically different backgrounds coming together in wholesome fellowship and literally "having a ball"! Like travelers to an unfamiliar country, people were learning new languages, breaking down barriers, and communicating with one another. The church was influencing the thinking of the artist, and the artist was enriching the life of the church!

An arts festival of this scope obviously can't be given every year, but less ambitious events maintain continuing communication with the artistic community. Each month, for example, a professional artist exhibits his work in a large hall adjacent to the sanctuary where members of the congregation gather after the worship service for coffee, conversation, and the perusal of books at the ever-popular book table. During these periods, the artist is present to chat about his work.

From time to time the church presents film festivals. These may feature serious commercial productions like *Death of a Salesman, Raisin in the Sun, Citizen Kane, Ballad of a Soldier,* or experimental films made by American, French, Italian, German, Polish, or Hungarian directors. Padanski's cryptic *Two Men and a Wardrobe* is an example. After the showing of these films, those present discuss their own interpretations of the message which the film seeks to convey.

Throughout the year the church's organist and music director, Michael J. Korn, presents organ recitals, large choral works performed by chorus and orchestra, chamber-type compositions for small choral groups, harpsichord, and stringed instruments, and recitals by artist pupils from local conservatories which give gifted young people an opportunity for public recognition.

Recently a little theater group, which had functioned in our community for twenty-five years, merged with the drama group in our church. As a result, the well-equipped stage in our auditorium is the scene of community productions which bring many unchurched people through our doorways. Hopefully, this kind of activity will help to wipe out the widespread misconception that the church today seeks to keep secular man from trespassing on its private preserve.

Here, then, are some of the ways in which a church can create passports which will make it easier and more attractive for people outside the church to cross the border into the unfamiliar, sometimes bewildering, ecclesiastical world that lies behind those bastille-like walls. But these tourists will come, Wayne, only if there is some indication that *their* language will be spoken, *their* customs respected, and *their* presence welcomed. Travelers are alike the world over; they shun those who treat them like aliens.

That's a challenge to us, isn't it? Remember how Moses reminds us that God "loves the sojourner, giving him food and clothing" (Deuteronomy 10:18), and that his people should "Love the sojourner therefore; for you were sojourners in the land of Egypt (Deuteronomy 10:19). Similarly, the writer of Hebrews points out that God's people "were strangers and exiles on the earth" who "are seeking a homeland . . . a better country" (Hebrews 11:13, 14, 16).

I hope you two sojourners are getting love and food from your European hosts. But if you're getting clothing, too, don't overlook the U.S. customs agents. They may not have read Deuteronomy or Hebrews recently!

Faithfully,

Ken

"Be a Fool for Christ's Sake!"

Dear Wayne:

You and Margaret have plodded through too many cathedrals! Otherwise you wouldn't have penned that postcard diatribe about miracles and the Holy Spirit. For such heresy, old-timers would sentence you to hellfire and damnation. Cool it, man; cool it!

I realize that miracles seem to hint of mysticism, the occult, the unworldly. And I know how easy and how tempting it is to dismiss such concepts simply by ridiculing them. But as an antidote, Wayne, let me share with you a *modern* miracle which illustrates the power of the Spirit. This miracle has been one of the most moving adventures in faith I have known. It involved travel, although the distance was only a few miles. It involved risk, with upper middle-class whites immersing themselves in a predominantly black ghetto culture. Initially it involved two girls, although ultimately it changed the lives of hundreds of people.

But let me start at the beginning!

At the time of the racial disturbances in Birmingham, Alabama, an interfaith, interracial rally was held one evening in our church sanctuary to hear a firsthand report by Rev. Andrew Young, chief strategist for Martin Luther King, with comments by other speakers. Among the six hundred people in the audience were two young women who came because they were interested in the problems of minority peoples.

The meeting was orderly and informative. Considering the emotion-laden subject matter, the mood was remarkably restrained. The two young women were impressed, first by the meeting itself, but also by the fact that a church was sufficiently concerned about this crisis to co-sponsor a gathering.

On Sunday morning the young women returned and worshiped with us. Again, they sensed in the church a willingness to face controversial issues and to seek ways of bringing about justice and reconciliation. When the time came to start a new class for people interested in church membership, both young women expressed a desire to take the six-weeks course. Since it was impossible for them and several others to attend the scheduled Sunday evening classes, I arranged to meet with them as a special group on Sunday mornings.

I still remember that initial meeting, Wayne. One of the young women, a British-born pediatrician, told me: "I shan't be joining your church, for within a few months I plan to go to Africa to make available my services in a hospital there." The other young woman, a magazine editor for the United Church of Christ, also said she wouldn't be joining, since she planned to enlist in the Peace Corps. They were assured that there was no obligation to affiliate with our church and that their association with us, however brief, would be welcome. Little did I suspect the extent to which these young women would have an impact on the future course of our stewardship. Typically, I was thinking more about how *we* might influence *them*. Too often this is exactly how the church regards the world; it is our brother who needs *us* and not *we* who need our brother! Anyway, by the time they completed the course both young women decided to join the church, if only for a few months.

Then came word of a retreat at Kirkridge, aimed at exploring ways in which our church might better serve the people of a nearby under-privileged interracial neighborhood. The British-born physician was on a holiday in England, but her editor friend attended. During the discussions about mission she found herself beginning to ponder whether it *was* necessary to join the Peace Corps and travel thousands of miles in order to minister to people in need. Did her medical friend *have* to go to far-off Africa? Was there, perhaps, just as urgent a need for their services in Germantown? Might not more people support a project in some exotic land than would respond to a nitty-gritty need in some depressed neighborhood of an American city?

As a result of this retreat and discussion between the two young women and our ministers, a compelling urge to take action developed. Said the two girls: "If a small group can be formed to sustain us, we will leave our comfortable suburban apartment and move down into a blighted urban area where we can in time learn to know the people and find appropriate ways to minister to them."

And that, Wayne, was the mustard-seed which led to the formation of the Covenant Group, consisting of the two young women, two of our ministers and their wives, and two lay couples from our church. Meeting weekly in various homes, studying Ephesians as a means of focusing attention on the biblical word and, through the sharing of prayer, striving to become sensitive to God's direction, the group began to evolve the terms of a covenant. As finally reduced to writing, it provided the following commitment:

> We are seeking to be God's instrument in his world. In our search we make this covenant. It binds each of us to the other in the name of Christ. We do this because we believe that one way we can see clearly God's purposes for us and Christ's power in us is through our unconditional commitment to love one another. We do this because we seek together to hear God's Word for today's world and to act on that Word. We do this because we believe that a Christian discipline needs to be specific. Thus we have mutually agreed to:
>
> Pray for each other every day.
>
> Study selected passages from the Bible every day.
>
> Meet together once a week for worship and study, sharing our lives with each other.
>
> Seek the direction of a Christian mission in Germantown.
>
> Make a monthly financial contribution to the mission.
>
> Give whatever is required of our time and talents and resources to the mission.
>
> Open ourselves to every possibility of ecumenicity in the mission.
>
> Participate in and be sustained by the life of First Methodist Church.
>
> Sanctify these mutual commitments by sharing together in the sacrament of the Lord's Supper.

This covenant was embodied in a brief liturgy and affirmed weekly in the group's worship service. Once monthly, an improvised offering basket was passed from person to person, and each member contributed the amount he or she had covenanted to give. The total came to $165.

The first opportunity to "open ourselves to every possibility of ecumenicity in the mission" was not long in coming. A Roman Catholic friend of the pediatrician, hearing of the project, was so intrigued with the idea that she proposed that she contribute fifty dollars monthly. After much soul-searching by the Covenant Group, an answer was dispatched. The offer was deeply appreciated, but in view of the needs which undoubtedly existed in her local area, she might, on reflection, prefer to contribute this amount closer to home. Back came the polite but firm decision: "I am already giving generously here; this is an 'extra' because I want to have a stake in your endeavors." This contribution, then, became the forerunner of many ecumenical gifts of time, talent, and money.

In the meantime the Covenant members, guided by an alert, black real estate man from our congregation, toured the depressed area inspecting available houses. Almost at the outset, the group decided it should buy a property and not rent one, for buying would be an act of faith, signifying to the community that this would be no short-lived experiment, but an effort to sink roots into the neighborhood. In a remarkably short time a house was found which providentially offered facilities that were unusual for such a section of town. On the first floor was a 28-foot living room, large enough to accommodate groups of adults or children. Adjoining it was a bathroom, a dining room which could become a medical office, and a kitchen. On the second floor were three rooms, a second bath, and a kitchen-dinette. A third floor provided two additional small rooms. The house was in deplorable condition, but structurally sound. In the rear was a yard, big enough for a play area or for off-street parking.

Although funds were limited, another act of providence solved the financing problem. Hearing of the project, a woman physician, also a member of our church, volunteered to lend the group five thousand dollars, interest-free, and repayable at the rate of one hundred dollars monthly. Quickly, some computations were made. Then the good news was announced. The amount being contributed by members of the Covenant Group would cover the repayment of the loan, the taxes, and the monthly charges for utilities, as well as insurance and minor repairs. It was a deal!

With the completion of settlement, the group legally owned what was to become known as "Covenant House." Just three months had elapsed since the ten members of the Covenant Group had held their initial meeting, a period barely long enough for most ecclesiastical boards to conclude that a scheme as harebrained as this was much too impractical to merit further consideration. Collectively, the Covenant Group virtually pinched itself to make certain it wasn't dreaming. It wasn't. The arrival of the initial tax bill convinced the most starry-eyed of the harsh realities of property ownership.

Now came evenings and weekends of backbreaking labor as members of the group scraped, sanded, painted, and in other ways transformed the grimy second floor into an attractive apartment. In this toil of love they received unsolicited but welcome assistance in the form of work and funds. Such energetic activity until midnight and later by this motley crowd of middle-class white interlopers naturally attracted considerable attention of curious neighbors. One woman who came to see what was going on asked the two questions which were to be raised again and again: "Are you girls actually going to live here?" and "Do you mean to say you've actually bought this house?" When answered in the affirmative, the neighbor shook her head unbelievingly. "My God!" she exclaimed, with more feeling than reverence. "Maybe there's hope for this neighborhood, after all. I'm going home and mix me a highball!"

The telephone installer was equally curious. "Why," he asked, "are you girls moving into a dump like this?"

"Because," replied the young physician in her clipped Hyde-Park accent, "I am not primarily concerned about making money. I am more interested in trying to help people."

His pliers clattered to the floor. "God! *That's* idealism!"

I'm sure, Wayne, that at this stage most of those who contacted us were sure we were out of our minds. But doesn't the Christian faith challenge us to be "fools for Christ's sake"?

Actually, the visiting neighbor who went back home to mix a highball really had put her finger on the crux of the situation. Maybe there *was* hope for the neighborhood! Clearly, it was at a crossroads. A few houses had been renovated and were neat and attractive. The great majority were run-down but *could* be repaired. Others, boarded up and fair game for vandals, were beyond reclaiming. A junk yard, a few littered vacant lots, and several nondescript manufacturing ventures gave the area the kiss of death. But just a little community pride, a little willingness on the part of whites and blacks to coexist in some semblance of neighborliness, might make the difference.

To occupy the second-floor apartment the girls moved some fifteen miles from their former suburban location. But psychologically and culturally, the transition might as well have spanned a continent. For, clearly, they were foreigners in an unfamiliar land. Their dress, their way of life, the British-born doctor's speech, and the little German-made automobiles they drove were all outward signs of inner differences. The neighborhood was wary, suspicious. Why were they here? What were they up to? Who were the others who descended on the house, filling the driveway with their motorcars, dashing in and out with bundles, and holding meetings which often didn't end until midnight? Why were there sounds of hymn singing and the uproarious laughter of people who seemed almost drunk, in their boisterous merrymaking?

Had a social service agency moved in, the mystery would have soon been dispelled. A large sign would have been erected, identifying the house. Publicity in the local papers would have explained that the agency was girding itself to help the poor. Paid workers on a nine-to-five work schedule would have pounded on doors, surveying the populace, and filling out printed forms. Then, at five-fifteen, they would have vanished from the scene and returned to the comfort of their suburban homes, leaving the house shut up, dark, and uninhabited.

But the girls were there not to work *on* people but essentially to become their neighbors. They were in a strange land, and they knew it. They couldn't even speak the language, let alone understand the customs. Accordingly, they undertook no activities, other than living at the house, smiling at people whom they passed on the street, shopping at the corner store, and getting to know the nice woman who ran it. All the while they were listening attentively to everything they could hear.

However, there lived on the street not just adults, but children—scores and scores of them, as many as ten to a family. And, being children, they were without timidity, suspicion, or prejudice. Into the rear yard they ran to play. But to their surprise, no one chased them out. Instead, the pretty young woman who returned each afternoon after teaching at the medical-college hospital actually played with them. The transition from yard to house was accomplished with childish speed and directness. "Miss Jennifer, can we all have a club? Meet in your house, maybe? Can we, Miss Jennifer? Can we? Say 'yes,' Miss Jennifer! Say 'yes!'"

And Jennifer said, "Yes!"

That, Wayne, was the real breaching of the barrier which surrounded Covenant House. For now that youngsters were beginning to use the big room on the first floor for their club, mothers no longer could look upon the place with hostility. Maybe these strange new neighbors *were* harmless, after all!

The club members needed toys, games, and books, and these began to appear on the scene. They also needed help in reading, as well as guidance in how to get along with one another without mayhem. Within months, two activities were launched in response to these grass-roots needs. One, a nursery school three days a week for preschool children, was supervised by an accredited teacher which the Covenant Group employed. A neighbor served as an assistant. The other activity, a tutoring program on a scheduled one-child-to-a-tutor basis, soon involved not only members of the Covenant Group but also many volunteers. These were people from our church, from other churches, from colleges and nursing schools, and various other individuals, including a Roman Catholic priest.

110

As work with the children continued to expand, dialogue with their parents gradually developed. An occasional meeting of mothers served not only to acquaint them with "The House" and its people but also to break down barriers between neighboring families. Parties were given for the children. Older youths were taken on weekend outings to nearby playgrounds and parks, to the zoo, and to downtown historic spots. Some of these city children had never been more than a few blocks from their homes; they had never ridden on a bus, been in a subway, or seen a department store.

As minor mishaps involving children occurred in the neighborhood, frantic dashes to the door of Covenant House were made because "Miss Jennifer, she's a doctor; she can fix it up!" Soon it became clear that the time had come for the launching of a medical practice. It was then that the doctor's "shingle" went up, and the children and their mothers came. They were charged a fee, for they were not looked upon as charity patients. When necessary, however, the fee was reduced or even waived. Rapidly the practice grew as well as knowledge of the problems, fears, and frustrations of the patients and their families. Now Miss Jennifer was becoming not merely a neighbor, but the confidante of the weary and heavy-laden who often did not know which way to turn for help. Thus, in addition to dispensing pills, capsules, and "shots," Jennifer began to serve as a referral and resource person. She marshaled available help to get the gas turned on again in that cold, dank dwelling down the street, asked a young attorney to check on the legality of a shady contract, helped a "client" to get the withheld relief check which rightfully was hers, or quietly paid an emergency bill from the modest funds set aside by "The House" for that purpose. In these complex human relationships she soon learned the truth of the biblical maxim to be "wise as serpents and innocent as doves."

Speaking of the Bible, Wayne, I should point out that as these various ministries evolved, the Covenant Group continued to meet, but for practical reasons, on a biweekly basis. Sitting together in a small room on the second floor of Covenant House, studying passages from the Bible, with children yelling in the street below, dogs barking, the raucous blasts of automobile horns, the distant wailing of police sirens, the peremptory pealing of a doorbell hinting at a medical emergency—served to create a fascinating dichotomy: The quaint, other-worldly message from two thousand years ago mixed with the strident turbulence of this twentieth-century metropolis. Yet that message spoke such incisive truths and chronicled problems and needs so similar to those at the doorstep, that

111

the reader gleaned from the pages not merely a summons to "get with it," but a sense of the direction in which he should move. We found our study of the Bible to be more fruitful, more relevant than ever before. It was as though the mission of the House gave the words new dimension and depth.

Our Covenant meetings also gave us an indescribable sense of closeness. Each person in the room felt bound to one another, sharing an affection which made us seem members of one family, as indeed we were.

Because of our contacts with the neighbors on the street, we found ourselves replacing old clichés about the underprivileged with fresh evaluations. No longer could we swallow the oft-heard generalizations that "those people are a shiftless lot, lazy, anxious to chisel, and if only they'd get off their bottoms, they could make a go of it, like I have." That simply wasn't the case with many of these people. There was the woman, for example, who was given some money during an emergency and thereafter came weekly to Covenant House to do the cleaning, because she wanted to repay the help she had received. There was the mother who brought her child for medical treatment and when admonished by Dr. Jennifer for not bringing the child sooner, in view of the seriousness of her condition, explained: "But I was waiting to get the money first!"

In other words, Wayne, this "adventure in faith" taught some of us middle-class folk that human dignity should be *everybody's* birthright. And it taught us that personal involvement in mission helps people to become more human and understanding, in a way that won't come about if, instead, we simply pay more tax dollars and make larger charitable contributions to enable professionals to administer relief. The poor need more than cold, hard dollars, important as they are. They need, too, the warm touch of concerned people who are willing to listen, care, help, and offer friendship.

Financial help grew in scope and generosity as word about Covenant House spread and as we incorporated and were granted tax-exempt status. Many individuals sent gifts of money, medical supplies, clothing, and equipment. A contribution of a hundred dollars from an American teacher in far-off Nigeria dramatized the truth that missions in America are no less authentic than missions abroad. Contributions also came from school children, church school classes, parish churches (including generous giving by our own church), church boards, and several philanthropic foundations. Conversely, Covenant House for several years has made a modest monthly contribution to C.F.L.A. (Catholics for Latin America) as an expression of fellowship with, and token support for, the work of a sister group in underprivileged urban areas of the Southern Hemisphere. Visitors to Covenant House have included ministers, teachers, professors, editors, writers, priests, members of religious orders, seminarians, and theologians from many parts of the United States. No less a celebrity than Bishop John *(Honest to God)* Robinson, of England, was among the visitors.

A more recent innovation in service to the neighborhood, Wayne, was the opening of a Planned Parenthood service, staffed by a certified gynecologist, a nurse, and a receptionist. The only facility of its type in an area with a teeming population in excess of 200,000, this operation is expected to expand as its services become more widely known. From it has evolved training courses for mothers and a beginning of family counseling in the homes of the area. Also, two additional physicians now serve the growing medical practice on a part-time basis.

In 1967, the Covenant Group disbanded, turning over the responsibility for running the House to a board composed of many of the original covenanters, plus dedicated people working closely with the various programs, including several black residents of the neighborhood who are providing invaluable guidance. The disbanding of the Covenant Group was not without much debate and trauma. It was necessitated, however, by the increasing time needed during each meeting to plan and administer the expanding programs of the House, which made it difficult, if not impossible, to continue the former schedule of worship, Bible study, and prayer. Significantly, many in the group have resumed this type of inner spiritual renewal and growth in some other context.

The most significant development of all, however, is taking place as I write this letter. With the resurgence of black power and the legitimate quest of black people for a personal and ethnic sense of identity, our black friends have indicated a desire to play a leading role in the policy-making and the program direction of Covenant House. They have not suggested white withdrawal. They welcome continuing participation of white leadership in the areas of finance and fund-raising, and white assistance in tutoring, teen-age youth programs, and other activities. But they rightfully hope to see Covenant House become a community-owned, community-operated venture, in which they have the greatest stake and to which they contribute time, talent, and as much money as they can spare.

Far from feeling threatened, the Board of Covenant House hailed this as an encouraging evolution in black maturity and, incidentally, in our own evolving white middle-class maturity! For basically we trust and feel genuine affection for our black colleagues, and they seem to reciprocate our warmth. Interestingly enough, after almost four years, this development coincided with a decision by Dr. Jennifer to move from Covenant House to a nearby place where she could have a modicum of privacy, yet continue her medical practice and her other responsibilities at The House.

This change in management is being accomplished by several innovations. First, a neighborhood advisory board has been formed, which determines on a grass-roots basis what services the community desires and needs. The Board of Directors then copes with the problem of setting up and financing the new program. Second, each program is directed by a community leader who serves either on the Advisory Board or on the Board of Directors. Third, the proliferation of activities is now coordinated by a part-time paid director from the neighborhood who heads the Advisory Board and serves on the Board of Directors. This woman, incidentally, has tremendous leadership capability. She is creative, tactful, dedicated, and accepted by the community. How surprised we were to discover, during a casual conversation, that she has a fine arts degree from the Chicago Art Institute! She is an impressive answer to those who cynically assert that there is no real leadership in the black community.

To indicate the sense of responsibility and judgment that these people exercise, let me tell you of their reaction to the youthful head of a militant black organization who recently strode into Covenant House and began to ask peremptory questions.

"Who runs this place?" he demanded haughtily. "I want to know when you're having your next meeting. I want to attend. I question whether you're representing the black community. I believe we should have a hand in running this place."

The black coordinator of activities replied: "You better leave, man. This is our place, and it's a private activity. And we're in charge. We aren't afraid of you, and we're not about to be pushed around. So goodbye."

The young militant left.

Today, Wayne, our Covenant House budget is $36,000, quite a contrast to the original annual pledge of $1,980 by the Covenant Group. Plans for augmented medical service will soon require the use of all the space in the house. When someone suggested the purchase of an additional house for the nursery school, library, and other activities, how thrilled I was with the response: "Let's not make the mistake so many churches have made and saddle ourselves with real estate."

Instead, we are arranging to lodge the activities in nearby facilities, renting space in churches or other buildings as needed. Not only will this be flexible and economical, but, more important, it will spread the influence of Covenant House throughout the neighborhood, making it less a "place" and more a "community program."

Covenant House, Wayne, has been one of the most exciting "adventures in faith" I have ever known, and I thank God for the privilege of being a part of it. I believe that Florence Allshorn had in mind projects like Covenant House when she wrote:

> You and I are to collaborate with God to make the world a better place. Our calling is not primarily to be holy . . . but to work for God and for others with Him. Our holiness is an effect, not a cause; as long as our eyes are on our own personal whiteness as an end in itself the thing breaks down. God can do nothing while my interest is in my own personal character—He will take care of this if I obey His call. In learning to love God and people as He commanded us to do, obviously your sanctification cannot but come, but not as an end in itself. If we are to collaborate with God in what He wants done, we must become like Him—and if we are set to do that, obviously the trends of laziness, pride, self-will, unintelligence, and any coldness of love must go. They are in the way of my obeying so they must go.*

Although at the time when each step was being taken in our Covenant House pilgrimage we couldn't honestly say that we could discern God at work, in retrospect, it is clear that the Holy Spirit *was* at work. How else could such a remarkable series of coincidences have enabled us to do so much in so short a time? Often we can see him only as we look back and know that he was there. When we look ahead, we must *trust* that he is there, leading us.

If your itinerary is accurate, Wayne, this letter should reach you in London at the Regent Palace Hotel. Whilst there (as our British cousins like to say) be sure to dine in The Carvery on the main floor. As the name implies, you pick up fork and carving knife and slice what meets your fancy from an appetizing array of roasts of beef, lamb, pork, baked ham, and other goodies. Yes, you can go back for seconds, too, if you have the nerve. Sort of an epicurean's idea of heaven on earth!

In another few weeks you'll be back again in the States. How eager I'll be to hear from you and get a full report of your reactions to travel, be it abroad or "on mission."

Faithfully,

Ken

"The Life You Save May Be Your Own!"

Dear Wayne:

Your letter arrived this morning, and I can't begin to tell you what a moving experience it was to read it. Do you realize, Wayne, the radical change that has come over you during the two months that have elapsed since you went to Europe and returned? I doubt it. And I'm certain you have no conception of the change that *your* letters have made in *me,* for the experience of seeing your faith grow, Wayne, has given me new insights—a fresh awareness of how God works—courage to hope that I, too, may learn to subordinate self to service for others. That's how faith begets faith.

Apparently two incidents have taken place since last you wrote, minor incidents, some might say, but I sense that they have profoundly affected your outlook on life.

The first was the receipt of that note, shortly after you arrived in Zurich, from a member of your *koinonia* group. Apparently you had experienced one of the few dismal days of your European travels—a long drive through the fog, your wife's sudden illness, the doctor's warning that hospitalization might become necessary. As you sat in your hotel room in this unfamiliar land, with the rain beating against the windows and the illness of your wife a cause for concern, you were overwhelmed by a desolate sense of isolation. Then, noticing the letter with an American postmark which the concierge had handed you earlier, you opened it.

Dear Margaret and Wayne,

I am not one to write letters, but we had a meeting of our *koinonia* group last evening, and ever since then I have had an urge to send you a note. I don't know exactly why this should be, but anyway I phoned Mildred Russell early this morning to check on your ininerary.

What I want to tell you, really, is how much we all missed you at our meeting. Our assignment was the second chapter of Ephesians. Harvey led the discussion. You both became a part of our conversation after Harvey had read this passage: "And he came and preached peace to you who were far off and peace to those who were near; for through him we both have access in one Spirit to the Father. So then you are no longer strangers and sojourners, but you are fellow citizens with the saints and members of the household of God, built upon the foundation of the apostles and prophets, Christ Jesus himself being the cornerstone" (Ephesians 2:17-20).

Harvey pointed out that although Paul wrote this letter from prison, he continued to reflect a deep and abiding faith in God, and in spite of trials and tribulations, he always was thinking about the people of his churches and their welfare. At that point Dave spoke up and reminded us that you two were traveling, and although far away, remained very close to us in bonds of the spirit.

And so we have been praying daily for you both and looking forward to your safe return. The group has not been quite the same without you. Have a good time but do hurry back.

Affectionately,
Janet

After receiving such a letter, I can understand what you meant when you said, "I suddenly felt as though a great load had been lifted from me. For reasons I can't explain, my entire attitude changed. No longer did the evening seem so dreary. For the first time I viewed Margaret's condition with optimism, and I ceased to feel alone. A strange peace came over me. We had dinner in the room, and that night I slept better than I had for a week."

I have a question for you, Wayne. When you read that letter, was it Janet or God who was speaking? And if it was God, would you have heard him if Janet had not written and become a vehicle for his voice?

Don't try to answer those questions, for in a sense they are rhetorical. But in another sense they are real questions, for they raise a basic point regarding our relationship to God and to our neighbor. As John Coburn has pointed out:

> You come to see each person as somehow bearing God to you. . . . Your response to the person will also be your response to God. In this way not only will you remain open to every human relationship, and be helped to treat each person as a bearer of God to you, but God will himself come to you intimately and directly and personally in and through all these relationships.*

I was a bit surprised that you did not question the coincidence which brought you such an appropriate note at the very moment of need. This is the sort of occurrence about which I never cease to marvel. I believe it was William Temple who said, "When you stop praying, coincidences stop." I suspect you can confirm this out of your own experience. Certainly this was a case in point. As you observed, the news that your *koinonia* friends were praying for you gave you a strange feeling of being sustained. How often people pray for others but fail to let the objects of their prayers know of their actions. And how unfortunate this is!

Recently I visited a businessman who prides himself on being hardheaded, a tough dealer, a man who doesn't let emotion interfere with his decisions. This boast, incidentally, is a tip-off that beneath his "mask" he's probably a rather emotional chap who craves affection. Anyway, this hard-boiled citizen interrupted our conversation at one point to yank open a desk drawer, pull out a letter, and wave it at me, saying: "I received this a month ago from one of your co-ministers. He wrote to tell us he liked a job our shop done for him, which was damned nice. But look what he said at the end of the letter. 'God bless you; I'm keeping you in my prayers!'" He shook his head as if in disbelief. "Think of it, Ken. The guy's praying for *me!*" Almost reverently he folded the letter and returned it to the sanctuary of his desk.

The other significant incident which you described, Wayne, also interested me. Upon returning to the States, you found a retreat scheduled, with places held open for you and Margaret. How thankful I am that you decided to go!

You tell me that you can't quite describe the unusual spirit that developed among those present. You say it was a sort of feeling you never had experienced before. Well, friend, don't try to explain it and above all, don't try to analyze it. Accept it and be grateful.

But it is significant that at the retreat a woman with whom you had scarcely talked came to you during one of the quiet periods and asked if she could speak with you privately. I was certainly impressed to read in your letter how you sat down with her and listened sympathetically while she described her childhood in a home torn by domestic strife, her efforts to escape by rushing into a marriage which failed to provide the happiness she craved, and how after her separation she had wanted to seek God's will for her life but instead, through timidity and self-pity, had drawn within herself and lost her best friends just when she most needed them. Apparently she turned to you because she sensed that you would listen, that you had compassion, and that you possessed a strength which she lacked. I gather this *really* amazed you, and as you began to talk to this young woman, you further amazed yourself by speaking with a newfound conviction of the importance of faith and of the need we all have to lose our preoccupation with self by becoming involved with the needs of others.

You must have had a tremendously meaningful conversation, for you tell me that a great change came over the young woman by the time you finished. She began to smile again and was exceedingly grateful for all that you had shared with her. Subsequent to this you felt a strange buoyancy which you can describe only by such words as elation, excitement, renewed confidence, and freedom from bondage.

In helping this young woman, Wayne, I just wonder if you might have discovered that the life you save may be your own! Or, as Roger Shinn has so penetratingly put it:

> Persons come to self-understanding only as they meet other people, accept responsibility, work and love, worship and pray, enjoy life, and enter into commitments. One way to learn about personality is to live as a real person. One way to understand humanity is to be human.*

Old-timers might say that you've had a "conversion experience." No doubt Dr. Shinn would update the language and observe that you've "become more human." But call it what you will, I sense that for the first time, in a deeply religious way, you've really begun to "feel." Prior to this, you consumed much energy and invited much frustration by striving to "think through." You were a Doubting Thomas, and surely you remember what Christ said as he allowed Thomas to place his finger where the nails had been and his hand where the wound had been inflicted: "Have you believed because you have seen me? Blessed are those who have not seen and yet believe" (John 20:29).

Unfortunately, Wayne, we live in a sophisticated age which is so enamored of science, so wedded to logic, so depersonalized by a kind of computer mentality, that we fail to realize that "how we feel" about *human* matters may ultimately determine whether we'll be permitted to stick around on this old planet and continue to worship at the godhead of technocracy. Paul Tournier points to the peril when he writes:

> Those scientists who are in the van of scientific progress are themselves afraid of the dangers inherent in it. After having made a public apology to the Japanese people, Professor Robert Moon, one of the nuclear physicists who helped to create the atomic bomb, declared to the Moral Rearmament assembly that this mortal danger would only be removed if we began to listen to what God was saying to us: "In our time," he added, "the Holy Spirit must take first place, and the intellect must come second."*

A significant point about your encounter with the young woman during the retreat was that she came to you. She took the initiative, but only because you were there, were approachable, and were willing to listen. She sensed in you a strength, a power, which she herself lacked. In a way, she was like the young R.A.F. pilot described by Florence Allshorn who said to a Christian:

> Don't try to help me or preach to me, or tell me what I ought to think yet. Don't work for my salvation, show me yours, show me it is possible, and the knowledge that something works will give me courage and belief in mine.*

I understand that many of those who work in the mission field today adopt this psychology. They don't set out to "convert the heathen" to Christianity, as did missionaries in bygone years, but instead they devote their lives to serving others, all the while awaiting the question, "Why are you here? Why are you so kind to me?" That has been the spirit of the people at our Covenant House, although on many occasions we debated whether we shouldn't come out and share our Christian faith with them. Were we perhaps "chicken" by keeping quiet? But each time, in the spirit of the R.A.F. pilot, we said to ourselves: "Let's not preach. Let's minister to others and hope that what we try to stand for may shine through." And the day did come when a woman asked of Dr. Jennifer: "Why are you here?" She handed her a copy of *The Christian Century*, pointing to an article in it about Covenant House. Silently, the woman read the piece. When she had finished, there were tears in her eyes. "Now I understand," she said softly.

Wayne, you tell me that you answered my initial letter and continued our correspondence throughout these many weeks only because I started out by admitting that the institutional church today often is a sick specimen of what a healthy company of the committed should be. You heartily seconded this view. But had I begun, you tell me, by giving you "that Jesus stuff," you'd have quit writing at the very outset.

My friend, I suspect your somewhat cynical reaction has some very basic theological validity. For, with certain notable exceptions, the church in our time has spoken with the unctuous voice of a public relations practitioner who seeks to enhance his client's image, while the church itself goes its own self-serving way, oblivious to the awful gap between its avowed principles and its shoddy performance. Even its words are archaic and meaningless. As H. Richard Niebuhr has put it:

> Our old phrases are worn out; they have become clichés by means of which we can neither grasp nor communicate the reality of our existence before God. . . . retranslation of traditional terms—"Word of God," "redemption," "incarnation,"

"justification," "grace," "eternal life"—is not possible unless one has direct relations in the immediacy of personal life to the actualities to which people in another time referred to with the aid of such symbols.*

Note how theologian after theologian stresses the need for "direct relations in the immediacy of personal life to the actualities" or, in less high-flown language, "personal involvement—service to the neighbor—servanthood—witness—commitment."

The new insights mean that churches simply have got to give up their preoccupation with selling themselves. They must cease packaging their religion in a colorful oversized carton which is found, on examination, not to contain the promised goodies but to be half empty and short-weighted. Sometimes, in my less rational moments, I fancy I can hear the church huckstering its wares via some monstrous television commercial concocted by an unholy alliance between Madison Avenue and denominational administrators. Listen!

Announcer (gentle voice, dripping with concern): Are you troubled, heavy-ladened, worried, unable to sleep at night? Does your conscience bother you? Do you feel you aren't getting ahead? Do you sometimes wonder if anyone loves you? (Voice takes on optimistic lilt) Then this message is for *you,* friend. Religion has given thousands of folks a *new lease on eternal life.* Just listen to the testimony of happy users!

Female Voice "A" (incredulously): Why, Marge, what a change in your appearance! I scarcely recognized you. You look so young, so relaxed, so radiant. How did you get rid of those circles under your eyes, those wrinkles, that worn, haggard look?

Female Voice "B" (brightly): Joan, I discovered a little thing called religion. Not just any old religion, but a very special vitamin-enriched religion called Christianity. And, Joan (excitedly), it's helped me to get rid of all those old feelings of guilt. And I haven't had to change my life one teeny bit! No tiring exercises. No wasting time with dull people. Just one little dose once a week, at 11 A.M., and you have no idea what a good feeling comes over you! Why, Joan, it's like a *new lease on eternal life!*

Male Voice "A" (approvingly): Jim, I've had my eye on you recently. Some new executive posts will have to be filled soon, and I've noticed a change in your attitude. Quite a change, my boy. You seem less hesitant—more decisive. And I like it. Would you want to tell your old boss what you've been up to?

Male Voice "B" (aggressively): Mister Jones, I've thrown off my inhibitions. I've found a great little success builder. Christianity, it's called. Teaches that with God, all things are possible. So I've adopted positive thinking. Whatever Amalgamated Industries asks me to do, I'll do, and without lint-picking questions. Sin on bravely, our minister tells me. Mister Jones, it's like a *new lease on eternal life!*

Female Voice "X" (whining): Florence, Bill and I are *so* depressed about this topsy-turvy world we're living in. We just don't know what to do. These minority people are getting so uppity; honestly, they just don't know their place anymore. And you should see the riffraff moving into our neighborhood! We've put our kids in a private school. But where can *we* escape to?

Female Voice "Y" (soothingly): Jennie, Clarence and I were upset, too. But we've found the solution. It's this vitamin-enriched religion called Christianity. It's great! We get it every week at our church sanctuary. The minister says a sanctuary should shut out the world and offer shelter. Well, *ours* does. And Jennie, it gives you the nicest feeling of security. Just like when we were young, Jennie. And you're with the *best* people. So try Christianity real soon. It's like a *new lease on eternal life!*

Announcer (unctuously): You, too, can have a *new lease on eternal life!* Religion does it, folks, but not just any ordinary religion. You need *Christianity,* which contains the magic ingredient G-O-D. Only *Christianity* has G-O-D in it, compounded according to a secret formula developed two thousand years ago. *Christianity* offers you health, wealth, and happiness. And remember, *only Christianity* gives you G-O-D!

Local Announcer (crisply): You can get *Christianity* locally at your nearest friendly church. Drop in some Sunday soon and ask the minister about it. He'll gladly show you the trial economy size. No obligation, folks, and a special money-back guarantee if you're not *more* than pleased. Positively NOT habit forming. Remember the name—*Christianity* with G-O-D in it. And see your friendly minister soon. You'll be glad you did!

Actually it isn't as bad as that, Wayne, thanks be to God. In fact, new life *is* bursting forth all over in Christ's church, on many fronts, and in ways that may herald the coming of a second reformation. But it's *not* bursting forth primarily because concerned people are worrying their

123

heads about promoting the success of the church as an institution. Instead, it reflects newly awakened Christians getting themselves involved in their everyday contacts with human beings, seeking to be open to their needs, as you were with the young woman on the retreat, and as we all must be to the thousands of little hurts and injustices which cry out for solution through concerted social, political, and economic action. And since the renewal of the church depends upon the renewal of its people, it will surely come in due time. But let's always remember, Wayne, that renewal —both personal *and* institutional—is a continuing phenomenon which must never cease. Let's remember, too, that as so-called atheists, non-believers, heretics, and religious drop-outs join with us in the struggle to extend justice, compassion, and reconciliation to all men, we are laying the groundwork for what an earlier generation called "evangelism." At some point these new friends will recognize the One they have been following.

This will be my last letter to you, Wayne. From now on I ask *your* help and *your* prayers. Far from "having it made," I daily face a continuing battle. If perhaps I have been of help to you in your thinking, now, in turn, I covet your help if I am to continue to grow. That, essentially, is our basic need for the Christian community. That is why I shudder when thoughtless church people, and sometimes thoughtless theologians, say that we can scrap the church and have a religionless Christianity. Apparently they do not realize that even during his last years in prison, Bonhoeffer helped to keep alive a sustaining community which was "the church," in a particularly powerful sense of the word. Therefore, let us today resolve to be helping one another, encouraging one another, and renewing one another in the faith. How? Through the church family. Through *koinonia*. Through prayer. Through a Christian style of life.

The daily temptations are many, and who among us is not exposed to them? One temptation is the feeling that we "have it made." This can quickly lead to self-righteousness, a false piety, a dangerous sense that we are somehow "religious." This is a time that calls for strict self-examination. We may be shocked when we realize that we probably haven't moved forward half as far as we think we have.

Another temptation is to become annoyed by the strident claims of those who threaten to change the status quo. As we hear these often frightening voices demanding radical action, we are likely to comfort ourselves by observing that they are simply fighting selfishly for *themselves,* but not for others, as we have fought for others. This temptation, too, requires objective self-examination. Perhaps these dissident voices are simply crying for justice. It could be that they only want their right, not a gift. At such times we must remember that peace without justice is not really peace, but merely an uneasy, inhuman, immoral truce.

Another temptation is to find that we no longer are responsive to the newer needs for change, but instead we hear ourselves saying: "Let's go slower. We're making good progress. The world really isn't so bad." We face this temptation increasingly as the years pass, and what formerly seemed to us to be radical becomes accepted as conventional. Then the words of Christ come mockingly to our ears, just as they came to Peter's, reminding us that we're seeing things through *man's* eyes, not God's. Then we begin to realize that our brother's view of life may be closer to God's view than is ours.

Still another temptation is the perversity of retrogression. We find our pride being wounded and our emotions aroused by the actions and words of others. Suddenly we "want out." We seek to escape involvement in the continuing stresses and strains of a fast-moving world, in spite of the likelihood that in just such situations we will be privileged to meet Christ. We are tempted to say, "Forget it!" Instead, we must continue to grow in understanding, forbearance, empathy, and grace, walking up the hard path to Christian maturity.

As I see it, a man might test himself by asking: "Do I feel like a good Christian or do I feel like a sinner?" If the former, he is still too tied to self. If the latter, he is closer to wholeness, which is only another meaning of holiness. This attitude should not imply self-disparagement, self-rejection, or self-pity. Rather, it acknowledges an understanding and acceptance of oneself on authentic, realistic terms. If we know ourselves to be sinners, never quite able to be the type of person we want to be, and can still like ourselves, respect ourselves, and live comfortably with ourselves, we then can relate to, and like, other sinners. I am always troubled by those Christians who are so critical of others (especially of those outside the church) that they fail to contemplate the harsh words of Christ:

> Woe to you, scribes and Pharisees, hypocrites! for you cleanse the outside of the cup and of the plate, but inside they are full of extortion and rapacity. You blind Pharisee! first cleanse the inside of the cup and of the plate, that the outside also may be clean (Matthew 23:25-26).

Those who condemn the Jews of Christ's day for not accepting him might reflect on how many of us Gentiles today accept only the more palatable portions of the food and drink this gracious host sets before us at his table.

One final word, Wayne! Don't be too concerned about motivation. Yours will never be, nor will mine, like Christ's, completely pure. It never will be generous and self-sacrificing to a degree that is unalloyed with self-interest. The same is true of humility. However, to compensate, a generous God has given us a sense of humor which we should turn upon ourselves at all times. The following may illustrate the point:

> I'm just a humble Christian.
> Cover me with sackcloth and ashes.
> I'm not very good, but at least I know I'm not very good.
> I'm not very smart, but at least I know I'm not very smart.
> Other people may be better.
> Other people may be smarter.
> But at humility I can beat them all.*

Just accept yourself as you are, a creature driven by many conflicting urges and desires, but loved by God in spite of your weaknesses. Be grateful that God loves you. The basis for positive thinking must never be insensibility to others or escapism. Rather, our possession of the knowledge of God's forgiveness, which frees us from constricting bonds, should enable us to act positively so that we can move forward freely in every effort to do his will. This is not easy. We must realize that we can never know the joy of discipleship without a willingness to bear the cost.

One last thought, Wayne! As I share it with you, please don't think me sacrilegious or frivolous; never was I more reverent, more earnest. It's this: If God entered history in the person of Jesus Christ, thereby giving man a glimpse of Deity more magnificent, more magnanimous, more manifest than he had ever known before, isn't it possible for God to re-enter history in *your* life, perhaps imperfectly, but with power to change its direction and to influence other men to open *their* lives to His presence?

Does all this sound like a sermon?

God forgive me. Who am I to preach?

Faithfully,

Ken

Notes

(The following references are the sources of the quotations marked with asterisks in the text.)

Page 14—Reuel Howe, *The Miracle of Dialogue* (New York: The Seabury Press, 1963).

Page 21—Gibson Winter, *The Suburban Captivity of the Churches* (Garden City: Doubleday & Company, Inc., 1961), p. 50.

Page 27—Elizabeth O'Connor, *Call to Commitment* (New York: Harper & Row, Publishers, Inc., 1963), p. 26.

Page 28—Martin Buber, *I and Thou* (New York: Charles Scribner's Sons, 1958), p. 12.

Page 29—Dietrich Bonhoeffer, *Life Together* (New York: Harper & Row, Publishers, Inc., 1954), pp. 27-28.

Page 30—Harry Emerson Fosdick, *The Living of These Days* (New York: Harper & Row, Publishers, Inc., 1956), p. 179.

Page 36—Austin Farrer, *God Is Not Dead* (New York: Morehouse-Barlow Co., Inc., 1966), pp. 66, 106, 114. Published under the title *A Science of God* (London: Geoffrey Bles, Ltd.).

Page 40—Salvador de Madariaga, "The Dangerous Lure of Parrotland," *Saturday Review*, April 22, 1967, p. 18.

Page 42—William Stringfellow, *A Private and Public Faith* (Grand Rapids: Wm. B. Eerdmans Publishing Co., 1962), p. 47. Used by permission.

Page 42—As quoted in Wilfred Grenfell, *A Labrador Logbook* (Boston: Little, Brown and Company, 1939), p. 17.

Page 59—Robert Raines, *New Life in the Church* (New York: Harper & Row, Publishers, Inc., 1961), p. 71.

Page 62—Bonhoeffer, *op. cit.,* pp. 37-38.

Page 67—*Ibid.,* p. 76.

Page 68—Paul Tournier, *The Meaning of Persons* (New York: Harper & Row, Publishers, Inc., 1957), pp. 42-43.

Page 69—George W. Webber, *God's Colony in Man's World* (Nashville: Abingdon Press, 1960), p. 59.

Page 73—*Corning Leader,* March 9, 1967.

Page 73—*Ibid.,* March 6, 1967.

Page 74—*Ibid.,* March 8, 1967.

Page 75—Bonhoeffer, *op. cit.,* p. 77.

Page 76—Thomas R. Kelly, *A Testament of Devotion* (New York: Harper & Row, Publishers, Inc., 1941), p. 79.

Page 81—George Caird, *Principalities and Powers* (Oxford: The Clarendon Press, 1956), pp. 80-81.

Page 83—Buber, *op. cit.,* p. 94.

Page 115—Florence Allshorn, *The Notebooks of Florence Allshorn* (London: SCM Press Ltd., 1957), pp. 27-28.

Page 118—John Coburn, *Prayer and Personal Religion* (Philadelphia: The Westminster Press, 1957), pp. 66-67. Copyright © 1957, by W. L. Jenkins, The Westminster Press. Used by permission.

Page 120—Roger Shinn, *Tangled World* (New York: Charles Scribner's Sons, 1965), p. 150.

Page 120—Tournier, *op. cit.,* p. 215.

Page 121—Allshorn, *op. cit.,* pp. 15-16.

Page 122—H. Richard Niebuhr, "Reformation: Continuing Imperative," *The Christian Century,* March 2, 1960, p. 251. Copyright 1960, Christian Century Foundation. Reprinted by permission.

Page 126—Robert McAfee Brown, ed., *The Collected Writings of St. Hereticus* (Philadelphia: The Westminster Press, 1964), p. 30. Copyright © 1964, by W. L. Jenkins, The Westminster Press. Used by permission.